CW00602001

CHIC LONDON

Written by
Beatrice Hodgkin

Illustrated by
Alain Bouldouyre

AUTHENTIK BOOKS
Les Editions du Mont-Tonnerre
4 bis Villa du Mont-Tonnerre
Paris XVe arrondissement

Published by The Globe Pequot Press
246 Goose Lane, P.O. Box 480
Guilford, Connecticut 06437
www.globepequot.com

© 2007 Authentik Books
www.authentikbooks.com

Produced in France by Les Editions du Mont-Tonnerre
Text and illustrations copyright © Wilfried LeCarpentier

Authentik® Trademark, Wilfried LeCarpentier
4 bis Villa du Mont-Tonnerre, Paris XVe arrondissement
www.monttonnerre.com

ISBN 978-0-7627-4633-0
First Edition

Printed and bound in China

AUTHENTIK®

LES EDITIONS DU MONT-TONNERRE
Founder and Publisher: Wilfried LeCarpentier
Editor at Large: William Landmark
Managing Editor: Caroline Favreau

AUTHENTIK CHIC LONDON
Restaurants, Wine and Food Consultant: Gérard Poirot
Project Editor: Nicola Mitchell
Project Editor and Writer: Jessica Fortescue
Copy Editors: Natasha Edwards and Susan Mann
Proofreader: Helen Stuart and Carly Jane Lock
Researcher: Jessica Phelan
Editorial Assistant: Jennifer Parker

Creative Director: Lorenzo Locarno
Artistic Director: Nicolas Mamet
Graphic Designer: Amélie Dommange
Layout Artist: Marie-Thérèse Gomez
Cover Design and Packaging: Nicolas Mamet
Cartographer: Map Resources
Map Illustrator: Kouakou
Pre-Press and Production: Studio Graph'M, Paris

GLOBE PEQUOT PRESS
President and Publisher: Scott Watrous
Editorial Director: Karen Cure

ACKNOWLEDGEMENTS
Special thanks to Marie-Christine Levet, Scott Watrous, Karen Cure,
Gunnar Stenmar, Gérard Paulin, Pierre Jovanovic, Jacques Derey,
Bruno de sa Moreira, Kelsey Hodgkin, Sophie Robinson
and Hermione Eyre

Uncover the Exceptional

The Authentik book collection was born out of a desire to explore beauty and craftsmanship in every domain and in whatever price bracket. The books describe the aesthetic essence of a city, homing in on modern-day artisans who strive for perfection and whose approach to their work is as much spiritual as commercial. Written by specialist authors, the guides delve deep into the heart of a capital and, as a result, are excellent companions for both locals and nomadic lovers of fine living. Their neat size, made to fit into a suit or back pocket, make them easy and discreet to consult, and their elegant design and insider selection of addresses will ensure that you get to the heart of the local scene and blend in perfectly with it. There is even a notebook at the back for some cerebral scribbling of your own. In all, Authentik Books are the perfect accessory for uncovering the exceptional, whether in the arts, fashion, design or gastronomy.

Wilfried LeCarpentier
Founder and Publisher

Contents

How to Use This Guide

Ever felt like jumping in a taxi at Heathrow airport and saying, "Take me to the centre of things!?" Well, this book does the work of a very knowledgeable cabbie.

Chic London consists of ten chapters of insider information on the most elegant, hippest and most happening spots around town. Discerning travellers with an eye for the unusual and a hankering after off-the-beaten-track treasures will find it an invaluable accessory. There's a selection of the best fashion and design stores, fine restaurants with fabulous settings, intimate cafés, cutting-edge cultural spaces, and the best spas in which to recover after all the fun.

The directory at the end of each chapter lists the addresses of the places mentioned, plus the details of other essential stops too numerous to mention in the chapters. The maps at the back of the guide cover the principal streets of central London. Use the map references following the addresses to find the general location of our listings.

The guide online

Using the **2D BAR CODE** below you can load all the addresses onto a mobile phone with Internet access. This unique aspect of the book enables you to travel extra light.

scan here

How to access content on your mobile phone

If your mobile phone has Internet access and a built-in camera go to

www.scanlife.com

Download the free software that allows your mobile phone to identify the bar code. Downloading takes less than one minute. Then go to your personal file icon which will appear on your phone's menu screen, and select the icon **Scanlife**. Next, point your camera at the 2D bar code. A sound confirms that the bar code has been recognized. You can then access the directories on your phone.

A KALEIDOSCOPE
OF STYLE

Tower Bridge, SE1

Previous page: Clifton Gardens, W9

L ondon has cultivated its own brand of chic. Fashion, the arts, music, nightlife – the city has a unique approach to all, and that's the secret to its allure. London is brilliant at shaking things up, mixing styles and inventing new ones. It's one of the most forward-thinking cities in the world, which can mean that it's hard for visitors, and even locals, to keep up. But there's no need to be overwhelmed.

01

Londoners may seem like hard-nosed, unfriendly folk on a mission to get on with their lives unhindered by elaborate forms of politeness. Unlike in France, for instance, sales assistants don't expect you to say "hello" and "goodbye and thank you" when you enter or leave a shop. But Londoners are secretly passionate about their city and their affected nonchalance belies a quivering curiosity and endless restlessness. True, they do emanate a certain *hauteur*, due to their pride in their capital but show a bit of chutzpah and style, and you'll quickly be accepted into the urban scene.

The key to London's urban chic is that it is deeply diverse. Its cultural mêlée embraces more than 50 ethnic groups, and the incessant buzz is in around 300 languages. Add to this the fact that London grew out of a collection of villages, each of which retains its sense of community, and you understand why the vibe is electric.

Fashion forward

In the west around **Notting Hill**, there are elegant boutiques catering to yummy mummies, while in the **East End** impossibly hip stylists and shabby chic individuals forage through vintage design and fashion warehouses and markets. Between these two areas lie **Mayfair**, **Kensington** and **Chelsea**, the places for luxury and high fashion, while a multitude of ethnic wares can be found in the increasingly presentable enclaves of **Dalston**, **Brixton** and **Shepherd's Bush**. That London accommodates with ease this kaleidoscope of style speaks volumes about its fascination with dressing up.

London designers take inspiration from saris, kaftans and tribal wear for their collections and, drawing upon the city's history, come up with Dickensian flare, nu-punk attitude, Swinging Sixties hip. They reinterpret old ideas in their own way. Effortless glamour the London way is not simply about donning this season's collection – it's about mixing designer and high-street, vintage and ethnic, and pulling off your own style.

Building with panache

01

London's cityscape is typically eclectic. Cast your eye along the Thames to get a sense of its architectural heritage. Grand, centuries-old edifices sit alongside run-down warehouses and brilliant, cutting-edge designs like Sir Norman Foster's Swiss Re tower, affectionately known as the Gherkin. The Houses of Parliament stare into the iris of the London Eye. The blockhouse architecture of the Southbank Centre faces the stately beauty of Somerset House. Each architectural creation has its spot, and none looks out of place. Landmark buildings are being revamped for new uses, including an old power station that is now the Tate Modern. Look at the 'It design spots' and you will see how the cityscape reflects London's melting pot of talent.

Eclectic tastes

Still mocked by those not in the know, London is in fact now one of the great food capitals of the world. As long as you know where to go, you'll find food and ambience that can rival not only the haute cuisine of Parisian establishments, but also the energetic fusion mixture of New York. London exploits its Asian, European, African, Australian, Polynesian and

The Routemaster
www.routemaster.org.uk

01

Russian (to name a few) influences, brilliantly, mixing and matching in a way that is simply unique. Perhaps The country's weaker gastronomic heritage has helped here, freeing up London to create trendy menus in smart surroundings that attract lively diverse crowds. Certainly the selection of gourmet meals and exotic drinks you can enjoy while relaxing in sumptuous surroundings is anything but identikit.

A sense of drama

The wealth of theatrical productions at the old Victorian theatres, complete with red velveteen chairs, chandeliers and gilding, encompass traditional, celebrated musicals as well as cutting-edge theatre, aided by a continuous sprinkling of big name actors from both sides of the Atlantic. Smaller independent theatres often produce artier, edgier goods while fringe theatres, including those in pubs, like the **Prince Albert** in Notting Hill and the **King's Head** in Islington, or in converted factories like Southwark's **Menier Chocolate Factory,** offer a particularly diverse selection of drama and comedy.

Made for walking

An invaluable tip is to get walking as London, like Paris, is best discovered on foot. It's best to stick to a specific area or two, rather than rushing about trying to fit everything in, since London is an enormous city.

The traditional London Black Cab service
www.londonblackcabs.co.uk

Make time for pampering and relaxation but be sure to branch off congested thoroughfares looking for the unusual; mosey away from the madding crowd along back streets, by the river, through the parks. The foreign visitor icons (black cabs, red buses, tube signs, blue plaques) give the city its basic flavour, but it's the pinch of secret ingredients, the ones you find off the beaten track, that really give the concoction its kick.

The scene via e-zine

The vibrancy and energy of the city can be exhausting, so ease yourself in before your arrival or stay up to speed using the tried and tested methods of the average Londoner: **e-zines.ldn.flavorpill.net**, **kultureflash.net** and **lecool.com/London** have their finger on the pulse, from bars to spas, restaurants to theatre productions via shops and cinema reviews.

Meanwhile the stylishly presented dose of snappy tips and insider information that arrives in your in-box courtesy of **Daily Candy** illuminates the world of boutique and bar openings, sample sales and niche fashion finds. As London is undeniably big, buzzing and constantly on the move, immediately knowing where to go to enjoy the best the city has to offer helps make your visit all that more memorable. The following chapters show you how.

HOT SHOPPING AND
SARTORIAL DELIGHTS

Pretty Ballerina
34 Brook Street, W1

Previous page: The Royal Arcade
Albemarle Street, W1

02

Despite the apparent predominance of chain stores, London is full of quirky, independent fashion and design boutiques that make shopping in the city a great escape. With just a little bit of rootling away from the main thoroughfares you will find specialist boutiques catering to every style and fashion whim. Each shopping area tends to have its own distinctive feel, be it smart and exclusive in Mayfair or vintage and thrifty in Spitalfields. The secret is to concentrate on one area at a time and browse at your leisure.

Sleek and chic Mayfair

Off cacophonous Oxford Street in the West End lies South Molton Lane, where you will find **Grays Antique Market**. Rows of stalls weave around one another under one roof and precious, unusual knick-knacks cry out for attention. Art Deco aficionados should keep their eyes peeled for hidden treasures, and **Vintage Modes** is a great stall for retro looks. The glittering boutique of **Butler & Wilson,** which has cornered the market in modern reinterpretations of classic jewellery, lies further up South Molton Lane, along with high-end shoe shops. Look out for

Smythson of Bond Street
40 New Bond Street, W1

Pretty Ballerina, which makes beautiful pumps in every colour and fabric imaginable. Further south, on Bruton Street, **Rupert Sanderson**'s sublime heels *(see page 28)*, with daffodil monikers for every model are a great investment for those who would like an elegant step up in the world. Sanderson's neighbours are **Stella McCartney** and perfumer **Miller Harris**, both invaluable places for dressing to impress.

Mayfair has also become a thriving area for concept stores. **Paul Smith** on Albemarle Street, **Marc Jacobs** on Mount Street (where you will find designs exclusive to this store) and **B Store** on Savile Row showcase limited editions, one-offs and innovative ideas. On Bond Street look up **Burberry** for understated British classics among other leading designers. Then branch off down Conduit Street to try on **Vivienne Westwood**'s nipped-in-waist designs and voluminous couture. Check out **Alexander McQueen** *(see page 28)* for va-va voom; **Smythson of Bond Street** for stylish stationary; and jeweller **Wright & Teague** for décolletage decoration.

Fenwick and **Liberty** *(see page 28)* are singularly elegant multi-concession shops. The fabrics and furnishing floor in Liberty are worth a trip in themselves. Invest in store vouchers: your plain old pounds sterling are converted into pleasingly weighty Liberty stamped silver coins.

Coco de Mer
23 Monmouth Street, WC2

Sassy Soho

Covent Garden and Soho both have a buzz about them that almost qualifies shopping here as a cultural activity. Shops are mingled with bars, businesses, theatres and clubs. Beneath saucy underwear emporium **Agent Provocateur** is cocktail bar **The Player**, and the pin-up style of the garments in the shop seems to call out for a devilish martini to complete the look. **Coco de Mer** (*see page 28*) is another sexily alluring underwear shop where performance prevails – virtually any fantasy can come to fruition with the goodies sold here. The diamante-studded crops are an accessory that'll whip you into the mood.

To add the prerequisite make-up needed to pull off sensual glamour, stop in at **Pout**. With both well-known brands and its own cosmetics line safely in store, it also offers a brilliant service whereby you can take in a favourite but discontinued item of warpaint, or indeed any piece of fabric that you'd like to copy in colour, and the store will create an exact match.

For the fashion-forward, **Concrete**, **Two See** and **Pineal Eye** show the way into hitherto unexplored fashion realms. **Blackout II** is aimed at the vintage crowd, but is no less bursting with one-off works of sartorial art. **Bang Bang** offers an interesting twist to

02

Fashion at a glance

Alexander McQueen: one of today's most brilliantly innovative designers known for his high-impact looks.

Bill Amberg: a leather god; there's nothing this man can't and hasn't done with hide.

Burlington Arcade: the longest and grandest of Mayfair's landmark shopping arcades oozes old-world glamour.

Coco de Mer: an alluring, luxe lingerie shop with silky drawers and diamante-encrusted crops.

Dover Street Market: the brainchild of Comme des Garçons' Rei Kawakubo is an exhibition space-cum-retail-extravaganza.

Liberty: the revamped multibrand store has innovative furnishings to die for.

Matches: a Notting Hill hot spot for discovering the latest, most sought-after designers.

Philip Treacy: hatter par excellence; anything but run-of-the-millinery.

Rupert Sanderson: sublime heels that are a rich investment for those who would like an elegant step up in the world.

Solange Azagury-Partridge: outré jewellery designs that sparkle with rock chic.

Steinberg and Tolkien: ornate, glamorous and rare vintage designs attract style mavens.

Topshop: a London institution known for affordable high-street fashion directly inspired by the latest catwalk collections.

secondhand clothes buying. Here you can sell your designer items, or swap them for stock you prefer, ensuring everyone's a winner.

For off-the-peg glamour **Koh Samui** is cocktail frock heaven. Arty types should make time to visit **Cosh UK** for its artists' prints and the creative library that is **Magma** – browsing through the reams of fashion, advertising and design books and magazines here is a frenzied cultural initiation. On the home design front, **Aram** focuses on contemporary furniture, including modern design classics, while **Bureau** has funky stationary. **Do Shop**, on Beak Street, has quirky things for the home you never knew you might need, at refreshingly accommodating prices.

Mellifluous Marylebone

Behind shopping heaven superstore **Selfridges**, Marylebone High Street and St Christopher's Place nurture an array of one-off boutiques. **Daunt Books** maintains a loyal following of glamorous literati, **Cologne & Cotton** prides itself on its sensual textures and scents for the bedroom, while **Rachel Riley**'s nod to a rural idyll in the urban metropolis forges ahead with traditional clothing for women and children. Laura Fuller's **Saltwater** and **KJ's Laundry** are two other fashion boutiques worth having a rifle through.

Steinberg and Tolkien
193 King's Road, SW3

At the north end of the street is the three-tiered converted stable occupied by the **Conran Shop** – invest here and you are one step closer to living a designer life. If retro classics are more likely to quicken your heart rate, a hop, skip and a jump over Marylebone Road is **Alfie's Antique Market**. Be it furniture, silver, jewels or clothes you're after, the hunt for real finds here is an adventure. Fashionistas need not come up for air until they discover vintage kingdom – **The Girl Can't Help It**. The name's a disclaimer of sorts; once there, they certainly won't be accountable for their actions.

The eclectic east

Out east, along Brick Lane and around Shoreditch and Hoxton there's been a surge in innovative, intriguing shops designing for the home, the wardrobe and everything in between. As you might expect in this part of town, the shops broadly fall into two categories – funked-up old classics and retro-inspired new classics.

Pushing the envelope with daring dexterity are **Hoxton Boutique**, a mirrored Studio 54-inspired fashion gallery, as well as **Start**, **Dragana Perisic** and **No-One**. If you wander along Brick Lane and its offshoots you'll find numerous new boutiques vying for your attention. In a vague attempt to keep abreast of the changes, drop into **Spitalfields Market**, which bursts with original stalls run by young designers. Open every day – Sunday is busiest, Thursday best for vintage and antiques and Friday for fashion and art – this should be the first stop for thrift diehards. Nearby, **Absolute Vintage**, **The Shop** and **Beyond Retro** lead the crowd with their huge warehouses crammed to the rafters. For accessories, **Black Truffle** showcases dynamic new designers. Not to be forgotten is the equally outré **Comfort Station**.

On the lifestyle frontline stand **Labour & Wait**, **Ella Doran Design**, **Mar Mar Co.** and **SCP**. Labour & Wait focuses on simple, timeless classics, which it imports from around the globe but all of which have a distinctly British feel. Industrial chic is the theme, but don't be fooled by the utilitarian design: the pink and cream enamel milk pans and horsehair body brushes are 1950s-style practicality with zing.

Northern lights

In more chichi Islington, Camden Passage, a pedestrianised alley running parallel to Upper Street, is home to a collection of small shops harbouring a huge number of undiscovered treasures. **Annie's Vintage Clothing** and **Cloud Cuckoo Land** sell fabulously ornate period costume, alongside an assortment of antiques shops and galleries bursting with bric-a-brac. On weekends, the street is home to an antiques market.

On Upper Street is **Castle Gibson**, a fantastic secondhand furniture shop. The proprietors restore neglected design classics, from wooden church pews to 1950s medical cabinets and Bauhaus-style suites. **Eccentricities** on Essex Road sells theatrical furniture for the home and garden. Mostly new, the designs are inspired by classic craftsmanship. **Aria** is focused on modern European design, and **Gill Wing** corners the home accessories market.

Adjacent to Gill Wing are the boutiques **Sefton** and **Labour of Love**. The former has two premises aimed at style-savvy men and women who like to mix edgy, fashion-forward designs with clean lines and slick presentability. The latter, together with nearby **Palette,** has a mix of upmarket vintage pieces and clothes and accessories by new designers.

Edging further north, there are some noteworthy shops in Hampstead and Primrose Hill whose leafy aesthetic and village-like warmth and intimacy cannot conceal the locals' pronounced style-consciousness. Hampstead's **Cochinechine** and **Question Air** have eagle-eyed buyers, so they display an ever-surprising collection of international designers, ranging from Day Birger et Mikkelsen and Malene Birger, to Jesire, Marc Jacobs, Sonia Rykiel and Yohji Yamamoto.

Theo Fennell
169 Fulham Road, SW3

Mixing established labels and emerging talents is an art, and Primrose Hill has a few secret gems that do it rather well. **Miss Lala's Boudoir** is a girl's dressing-up box filled with vintage jewellery, all manner of frilly, silky delights, plus some racy knickers. **Tallulah** in Islington is also a worthwhile bet – the silk handcuffs hold the promise of entertainment worth investing in. **Shikasuki** effortlessly mixes 1950s prom dresses and Ossie Clark gowns with contemporary pieces; **Studio 8** has perfected the art of selecting lesser known fashion lines that will have even the most penny-pinching delving into their purses.

Chichi Chelsea

If you are armed with a fan of credit cards, you will find Kensington, Chelsea and Knightsbridge are excellent shopping destinations. Dominating the retail skyline is **Harrods**; if it's chic, it's probably here. With food, furniture, couture and lingerie, this is an emporium to end all emporiums.

Up towards Brompton Cross, back to Sloane Street and along the King's Road and its tributaries, the vibe is more intimately exclusive. **Joseph** and **Whistles** stock timeless classics alongside interesting experimental designers. **Austique** prides itself on being every girl-in-the-know's stomping ground. **Mimi** is the place for complementary British, American and Italian designers, while **Bamford & Sons** is the stop for elegant, classic men's and womenswear. **Coco Ribbon** sells girly, boudoir-fabulous designs by the likes of Alice Temperley; **Lulu Guinness** focuses on 1950s inspired bags and shoes; **Kiki McDonough** and **Theo Fennell** are the Chelsea set's choice for fine jewellery. The ribbon and appliqué fantasyland, **VV Rouleaux** is a must-visit. **Cutler and Gross** is the place for specs – bejewelled, media-trendy, designer, and vintage: there's a frame for every face.

William Yeoward, **Katherine Pooley** and **David Linley** are the places for amazing craftsmanship and design on the home front, while the bedlinen and furnishing fabrics from **Designers Guild** come in a kaleidoscope of options for jazzing up modern living.

For wallpaper, **Cole and Son** and Neisha Crosland's **Ginka** take classic designs and give them a modern twist; Cole and Son's forte is flocked paper of the highest quality, in bold, wild colours. For linens and lace, the **Monogrammed Linen Shop** is a cornucopia of delights for the home. Also worth visiting is **Boyd** on Elizabeth Street, an inspiring space that reflects both Tracey Boyd's womenswear and her new home furnishings line.

The wild west

West London trendies and yummy mummies congregate in Notting Hill. Shopping here is nothing short of idyllic; Shops sit along tree-lined avenues, beside rows of artistically colourful houses. Aim to go to Portobello Market on a Friday, when the stalls sell more exclusive wares and there aren't three million people trying to walk in every direction, as there are on Saturdays.

Portobello Road has a number of shops worth seeking out. At **Olivia Morris**, DIY blank canvas shoes come with a set of paints for you to design your own pattern, and a clip on accessory for evening sparkle. Jasmine Guinness's shop for children, **Honey Jam**, has some natty toys, and **One of a Kind** has just that – vintage items you'd be hard pressed to find elsewhere. **Rellik**, at the end of Golborne Road is another favourite for secondhand gems. Nearby **Les Couilles du Chien**, nestled among all the Portuguese and North African cafés in the shadow of the Trellick Towers, is a real find, full of weird and wonderful antiques for the home.

On Ledbury Road and Westbourne Grove are wealth of original boutiques. **Alice and Astrid** stock delicate dresses and accessories, **Emma Hope** is the place to find the perfect shoe, while unique one-off items can be found at the aptly named **One**. Sweet cashmere

Myla
77 Lonsdale Road, W11

designs for every inch of the body are staples in **Brora**, and **J&M Davidson** excels in simple, elegant classics – its handbags come high on most discerning shoppers' wish lists. **Brissi** is brilliant for chic, French-inspired housewares, and in **Nicole Farhi**'s café, you can bask in the designer's style and imagine what it would be like to import the furniture lock stock and barrel into your own home.

Sleek and chic Mayfair

B Store
24a Savile Row, W1
⊖ Oxford Circus
(020 7734 0467
bstorelondon.com
⊕ 6-7/N9

Burberry
21 New Bond St, W1
⊖ Bond Street
(020 7968 0000
burberry.com
⊕ 6/M8

Butler & Wilson
20 South Molton St, W1
⊖ Bond Street
(020 7409 2955
butlerandwilson.co.uk
⊕ 6/M8

Fenwick
63 New Bond St, W1
⊖ Bond Street
(020 7629 9161
fenwick.co.uk
⊕ 6/M8

Grays Antique Market
58 Davies St, W1
⊖ Bond Street
(020 7629 7034
graysantiques.com
⊕ 6/L8

Marc Jacobs
24-25 Mount St, W1
⊖ Bond Street
(020 7399 1690
marcjacobs.com
⊕ 10/K10

Matthew Williamson
28 Bruton St, W1
⊖ Green Park
(020 7629 6200
matthewwilliamson.com
⊕ 6/M9

Miller Harris
21 Bruton St, W1
⊖ Green Park
(020 7629 7750
millerharris.com
⊕ 6/M9

Mulberry
41 New Bond St, W1
⊖ Bond Street
(020 7491 3900
mulberry.com
⊕ 6/M8

Paul Smith
9 Albemarle St, W1
⊖ Green Park
(020 7493 4565
paulsmith.co.uk
⊕ 11/M10

Pickett
32 Burlington Arcade, W1
⊖ Green Park
(020 7493 8939
pickett.com
⊕ 11/N10

02

Pretty Ballerina
34 Brook St, W1
⊖ Bond Street
(020 7493 3957
prettyballerina.com
⊕ 6/L9

Pringle
112 New Bond St, W1
⊖ Bond Street
(020 7297 4580
pringlescotland.com
⊕ 6/M8

Rupert Sanderson
33 Bruton Pl, W1
⊖ Green Park
(0870 750 9181
rupertsanderson.co.uk
⊕ 6/M9

Smythson of Bond Street
40 New Bond St, W1
⊖ Bond Street
(020 7629 8558
smythson.com
⊕ 6/M8

Sleek and chic Mayfair

Stella McCartney
30 Bruton St, W1
⊖ Green Park
(020 7518 3100
stellamccartney.com
⊕ 6/M9

Vivienne Westwood
44 Conduit St, W1
⊖ Oxford Circus
(020 7439 1109
viviennewestwood.co.uk
⊕ 6/M9

Wright & Teague
1a Grafton St, W1
⊖ Green Park
(020 7629 2777
wrightandteague.com
⊕ 10/M9

Sassy Soho

Agent Provocateur
6 Broadwick St, W1
⊖ Oxford Circus
(020 7439 0229
agentprovocateur.com
⊕ 7/O8

Bureau
10 Great Newport St,
WC2
⊖ Leicester Square
(020 7379 7898
⊕ 7/P9

Do Shop
47 Beak St, W1
⊖ Oxford Circus
(020 7494 9090
do-shop.co.uk
⊕ 6-7/N9

Aram
110 Drury Lane, WC2
⊖ Covent Garden
(020 7557 7557
aram.co.uk
⊕ 7/Q8

Coco de Mer
23 Monmouth St, WC2
⊖ Covent Garden
(020 7836 8882
coco-de-mer.co.uk
⊕ 7/P8

Koh Samui
65 Monmouth St, WC2
⊖ Covent Garden
(020 7240 4280
⊕ 7/P8

Bang Bang
9 Berwick St, W1
⊖ Tottenham Court Rd
(020 7494 2042
myspace.com/
bangbangexchange
⊕ 7/O8

Concrete
35a Marshall St, W1
⊖ Oxford Circus
(020 7434 4546
⊕ 7/N8

Magma
8 Earlham St, WC2
⊖ Covent Garden
(020 7240 8498
magmabooks.com
⊕ 7/P8

Blackout II
51 Endell St, WC2
⊖ Covent Garden
(020 7240 5006
blackout2.com
⊕ 7/Q8

Cosh UK
69 Berwick St, W1
⊖ Oxford Circus
(020 7287 7758
coshuk.com
⊕ 7/O8

Pineal Eye
49 Broadwick St, W1
⊖ Oxford Circus
(020 7434 2567
⊕ 7/O8

The Player
8-12 Broadwick St, W1
Tottenham Court Rd
0871 426 1996
7/O8

Pout
32 Shelton St, WC2
Covent Garden
020 7379 0379
pout.co.uk
7/Q8

Two See
17 Monmouth St, WC2
Covent Garden
020 7240 7692
twoseelife.com
7/P8

Mellifluous Marylebone

02

Alfie's Antique Market
13 Church St, NW8
Edgware Road
020 7723 6066
alfiesantiques.com
6/H6

The Girl Can't Help It
Alfie's Antique Market,
13 Church St, NW8
Edgware Road
020 7723 8984
alfiesantiques.com
6/H6

Rachel Riley
82 Marylebone High St, W1
Baker Street
020 7935 7007
rachelriley.com
6-7/L6

Cologne & Cotton
88 Marylebone
High St, W1
Baker Street
020 7486 0595
cologneandcotton.com
6-7/L6

KJ's Laundry
74 Marylebone Lane, W1
Bond Street
020 7486 7855
kjslaundry.com
6-7/L6

Saltwater
98 Marylebone Lane, W1
Bond Street
020 7935 3336
saltwater.com
6-7/L6

Conran Shop
55 Marylebone
High St, W1
Baker Street
020 7723 2223
conranshop.co.uk
6-7/L6

L'Artisan Parfumeur
36 Marylebone
High St, W1
Baker Street
020 7486 3435
artisanparfumeur.com
6-7/L6

Selfridges
400 Oxford St, W1
Bond Street
0800 123 400
selfridges.com
6/K8

Daunt Books
83 Marylebone High St, W1
Baker Street
020 7224 2295
dauntbooks.co.uk
6-7/L6

Mint
70 Wigmore St, W1
Bond Street
020 7224 4406
6/K8

Skandium
86 Marylebone High St, W1
Bond Street
020 7935 2077
skandium.com
6-7/L6

The eclectic east

Absolute Vintage
15 Hanbury St, E1
Liverpool Sreet
020 7247 3883
absolutevintage.co.uk
8/Z6

Ally Capellino
5 Calvert Ave, E2
Old Street
020 7613 3073
allycapellino.co.uk
4/Z5

Beyond Retro
110 Cheshire St, E2
Shoreditch
020 7613 3636
beyondretro.com
Off map

Black Truffle
74 Broadway Market, E8
Bethnal Green
020 7923 9450
blacktruffle.com
Off map

Comfort Station
22 Cheshire St, E2
Shoreditch
020 7033 9099
comfortstation.co.uk
Off map

Dragana Perisic
30 Cheshire St, E2
Shoreditch
020 7739 4484
draganaperisic.com
Off map

Ella Doran Design
46 Cheshire St, E2
Shoreditch
020 7613 0782
elladoran.co.uk
Off map

Hoxton Boutique
2 Hoxton St, N1
Old Street
020 7684 2083
hoxtonboutique.co.uk
4/Y4

Labour & Wait
18 Cheshire St, E2
Shoreditch
020 7729 6253
labourandwait.co.uk
Off map

Mar Mar Co
16 Cheshire St, E2
Shoreditch
020 7729 1494
marmarco.com
Off map

No-One
1 Kingsland Rd, E2
Old Street
020 7613 5314
no-one.co.uk
4/Z3

SCP
139 Curtain Rd, EC2
Old Street
020 7739 1869
scp.co.uk
5/Y5

The Shop
3 Cheshire St, E2
Shoreditch
020 7739 5631
Off map

Spitalfields Market
Brushfield St, E1
Liverpool Street
020 7377 1496
spitalfields.co.uk
8/Z7

Start
42, 59 Rivington St, EC2
Old Street
020 7739 3334
start-london.com
8/Y5

Northern lights

Annie's Vintage Clothing
12 Camden Passage, N1
⊖ Angel
(020 7359 0796
anniesvintageclothing.co.uk
⊕ 4/U2

Aria
295-7 Upper St, N1
⊖ Angel
(020 7704 6222
aria-shop.co.uk
⊕ 4/T2

Castle Gibson
106a Upper St, N1
⊖ Angel
(020 7704 0927
castlegibson.com
⊕ 4/T2

Cloud Cuckoo Land
6 Charlton Pl,
Camden Passage, N1
⊖ Angel
(020 7354 3141
⊕ 4/U2

Cochinechine
74 Heath St, NW3
⊖ Hampstead
(020 7435 9377
cochinechine.com
⊕ Off map

Eccentricities
46 Essex Rd, N1
⊖ Angel
(020 7359 5633
keithskeel.co.uk
⊕ 4/U1

Gill Wing
190 Upper St, N1
⊖ Highbury & Islington
(020 7226 5392
⊕ 4/T2

Labour of Love
193 Upper St, N1
⊖ Highbury & Islington
(020 7354 9333
labour-of-love.co.uk
⊕ 4/T2

Miss Lala's Boudoir
148 Gloucester Ave,
NW1
⊖ Chalk Farm
(020 7483 1888
misslalasboudoir.co.uk
⊕ 2/L1

Palette
21 Canonbury Lane, N1
⊖ Highbury & Islington
(020 7288 7428
palette-london.com
⊕ Off map

Question Air
28 Rosslyn Hill, NW3
⊖ Hampstead
(020 7435 9221
question-air.com
⊕ Off map

Sefton
196, 271 Upper St, N1
⊖ Highbury & Islington
(020 7226 9822
seftonfashion.com
⊕ 4/T2

Shikasuki
67 Gloucester Av, NW1
⊖ Chalk Farm
(020 7722 4442
shikasuki.co.uk
⊕ 2/L1

Studio 8
83 Regent's Park Rd, NW1
⊖ Chalk Farm
(020 7449 0616
⊕ 2/K1

Tallulah
65 Cross St, N1
⊖ Angel
(020 7704 0066
tallulah-lingerie.co.uk
⊕ 4/U1

02

Chichi Chelsea

Austique
330 King's Rd, SW3
⊖ Sloane Square
℡ 020 7376 4555
austique.co.uk
⊕ 14/H17

Bamford & Sons
31 Sloane Sq, SW1
⊖ Sloane Square
℡ 020 7881 8010
bamfordandsons.com
⊕ 10/K14

Boyd
42 Elizabeth St, SW1
⊖ Victoria
℡ 020 7730 3939
traceyboyd.co.uk
⊕ 10/L14

Coco Ribbon
133 Sloane St, SW1
⊖ Sloane Square
℡ 020 7730 8555
cocoribbon.com
⊕ 10/J14

Cole and Son
10 Chelsea Harbour
Design Centre, SW10
⊖ Fulham Broadway
℡ 020 7376 4628
cole-and-son.com
⊕ Off map

Cornucopia
12 Upper Tachbrook St, SW1
⊖ Pimlico
℡ 020 7828 5752
⊕ 15/N15

Cutler and Gross
16 Knightsbridge Green,
SW1
⊖ Knightsbridge
℡ 020 7581 2250
cutlerandgross.co.uk
⊕ 10/J12

David Linley
60 Pimlico Rd, SW1
⊖ Sloane Square
℡ 020 7730 7300
davidlinley.com
⊕ 2/K5

Designers Guild
277 King's Rd, SW3
⊖ Sloane Square
℡ 020 7351 5775
designersguild.com
⊕ 14/H17

French Sole
6 Ellis St, SW1
⊖ Sloane Square
℡ 020 7730 3771
frenchsole.com
⊕ 14/J-K15

Ginka
137 Fulham Rd, SW3
⊖ South Kensington
℡ 020 7589 4866
neishacrosland.com
⊕ 13/F17

Harrods
87 Brompton Rd, SW1
⊖ Knightsbridge
℡ 020 7730 1234
harrods.com
⊕ 10/I13

Joseph
74 Sloane Ave, SW3
⊖ South Kensington
℡ 020 7591 0808
joseph.co.uk
⊕ 14/I15

Katherine Pooley
160 Walton St, SW3
⊖ South Kensington
℡ 020 7584 3223
katherinepooley.com
⊕ 14/I14

Kiki McDonough
77c Walton St, SW3
⊖ South Kensington
℡ 020 7581 1777
kikimcd.com
⊕ 14/I14

Lulu Guinness
3 Ellis St, SW1
⊖ Sloane Square
(020 7823 4828
luluguinness.com
⊕ 14/K14

Mimi
309 King's Rd, SW3
Oxford Circus
⊖ Sloane Square
(020 7349 9699
mimilondon.co.uk
⊕ 14/H17

Monogrammed Linen Shop
168 Walton St, SW3
⊖ South Kensington
(020 7589 4033
monogrammed
linenshop.com
⊕ 14/I14

Selina Blow
1 Ellis St, SW1
⊖ Sloane Square
(020 7730 2077
selinablow.com
⊕ 14/K14

Steinberg and Tolkein
193 King's Rd, SW3
⊖ Sloane Square
(020 7376 3660
⊕ 14/H17

Theo Fennell
169 Fulham Rd, SW3
⊖ South Kensington
(020 7591 5000
theofennell.com
⊕ 13/F17

VV Rouleaux
54 Sloane Sq, SW1
⊖ Sloane Square
(020 7730 3125
vvrouleaux.com
⊕ 14/K14

Whistles
31 King's Rd, SW3
⊖ Sloane Square
(020 7730 2006
whistles.co.uk
⊕ 14/H17

William Yeoward
270 King's Rd, SW3
⊖ Sloane Square
(020 7349 7828
williamyeoward.com
⊕ 14/H17

02

The wild west

Aimé
32 Ledbury Rd, W11
⊖ Notting Hill Gate
(020 7221 7070
aimelondon.com
⊕ 5/C8

Alice and Astrid
30 Artesian Rd, W2
⊖ Notting Hill Gate
(020 7985 0888
aliceandastrid.com
⊕ 5/C8

Brissi
196 Westbourne Grove, W11
⊖ Notting Hill Gate
(020 7727 2159
brissi.co.uk
⊕ 5/C8

Brora
66 Ledbury Rd, W11
⊖ Notting Hill Gate
(020 7229 1515
brora.co.uk
⊕ 5/C8

Cath Kidston
8 Clarendon Cross, W11
⊖ Holland Park
(020 7221 4000
cathkidston.co.uk
⊕ 9/A10

Celia Birtwell
71 Westbourne Park Rd, W2
⊖ Westbourne Grove
(020 7229 7673
celiabirtwell.com
⊕ 5/A7

The wild west

The Cross
141 Portland Rd, W11
⊖ Holland Park
© 020 7727 6760
⊕ 9/A10

Diane Von Furstenberg
83 Ledbury Rd, W11
⊖ Westbourne Grove
© 020 7221 1120
dvf.com
⊕ 5/C8

Emma Hope
207 Westbourne Grove, W11
⊖ Notting Hill Gate
© 020 7313 7490
emmahope.co.uk
⊕ 5/C8

Honey Jam
267 Portobello Rd, W11
⊖ Ladbroke Grove
© 020 7243 0449
⊕ 5/A6

J&M Davidson
42 Ledbury Rd, W11
⊖ Notting Hill Gate
© 020 7313 9532
jandmdavidson.com
⊕ 5/C8

Les Couilles du Chien
65 Golborne Rd, W10
⊖ Ladbroke Grove
© 020 8968 0099
lescouillesduchien.co.uk
⊕ 5/A6

Myla
77 Lonsdale Rd, W11
⊖ Notting Hill Gate
© 020 7221 9222
myla.com
⊕ 5/B8

Nicole Farhi
202 Westbourne Grove, W11
⊖ Notting Hill Gate
© 020 7792 6888
nicolefarhi.com
⊕ 5/C8

Olivia Morris
355 Portobello Rd, W10
⊖ Ladbroke Grove
© 020 8962 0353
oliviamorrisshoes.com
⊕ 5/A6

One
30 Ledbury Rd, W11
⊖ Notting Hill Gate
© 020 7221 5300
only0ne.com
⊕ 5/C8

One of a Kind
253 Portobello Rd, W11
⊖ Ladbroke Grove
© 020 7792 5284
⊕ 5/A6

Rellik
8 Golborne Rd, W10
⊖ Ladbroke Grove
© 020 8962 0089
relliklondon.co.uk
⊕ 5/A6

The Rug Company
124 Holland Park Av, W11
⊖ Holland Park
© 020 7229 5148
therugcompany.info
⊕ 9/A10

Temperley
6 Colville Mews, W11
⊖ Notting Hill Gate
© 020 7229 7957
temperleylondon.com
⊕ 5/C8

Virginia
98 Portland Rd, W11
⊖ Holland Park
© 020 7727 9908
⊕ 9/A10

Fashion at a glance

Alexander McQueen
4 Old Bond St, W1
⊖ Green Park
℡ 020 7355 0088
alexandermcqueen.com
⊕ 11/N10

Bill Amberg
21 Chepstow Pl, W2
⊖ Notting Hill Gate
℡ 020 7727 3560
billamberg.com
⊕ 5-9/D9

Burlington Arcade
Piccadilly, W1
⊖ Piccadilly
burlington-arcade.co.uk
⊕ 11/M11

Coco de Mer
23 Monmouth St, WC2
⊖ Covent Garden
℡ 020 7836 8882
coco-de-mer.co.uk
⊕ 7/P8

Dover Street Market
17 Dover St, W1
⊖ Green Park
℡ 020 7518 0680
doverstreetmarket.com
⊕ 11/M10

Liberty
Great Marlborough St, W1
⊖ Oxford Circus
℡ 020 7734 1234
libertyoflondon.co.uk
⊕ 7/N8

Matches
60 Ledbury Rd, W11
⊖ Notting Hill Gate
℡ 020 7221 0255
matchesfashion.com
⊕ 5/C8

Philip Treacy
69 Elizabeth St, SW1
⊖ Victoria
℡ 020 7730 3992
philiptreacy.co.uk
⊕ 14/L14

Rupert Sanderson
33 Bruton Pl, W1
⊖ Green Park
℡ 0870 7509 181
rupertsanderson.co.uk
⊕ 6/M9

Solange Azagury-Partridge
187 Westbourne Grove, W11
⊖ Notting Hill Gate
℡ 020 7792 0197
solangeazagurypartridge.com
⊕ 5/C8

Steinberg and Tolkien
193 King's Rd, SW3
⊖ Sloane Square
℡ 020 7376 3660
⊕ 14/H17

Topshop
Oxford Circus, W1
⊖ Oxford Circus
℡ 020 7636 7700
topshop.com
⊕ 7/N8

02

See page 9
to scan the
directory

BESPOKE FASHION
AND CRAFTSMANSHIP

Ozwald Boateng
9 Vigo Street, W1

Previous page: Floris
89 Jermyn Street, SW1

L ondon is a haven for all things custom made, from underwear to three-piece worsted suits. Savile Row is an obvious starting place, especially for the gentleman dandy, but women's options abound, too: think softly crafted cashmere in a colour and size woven just for you. Nearby, St James's is bastion island of shops focused on goods, such as hats, cigars, umbrellas and country attire, that hark back to an era of quintessential Britishness.

03

Tailored living

Savile Row was originally developed as part of the Burlington Estate and was named after Lord Burlington's wife, Lady Dorothy Savile. But it was not until the 1800s that it really began to acquire its global reputation for tailoring. **Gieves & Hawkes**, at No.1, makes an impressive introduction to the street. You can buy ready-to-wear menswear here, but the store is identified with bespoke suits, and it's well worth investing in one if you can afford it.

Along the street, the various on-site ateliers each have their own forte, so do a little research before committing your cash. It's tricky to say who are the best as much depends on your personal rapport with the tailor and the kind of suit you need. As a guideline, cutters at the Row's founding father, **Henry Poole**, established in 1806, are known for their detailing and ornamentation, while the formality and rather Dickensian austerity of **Anderson & Sheppard**'s service expresses itself in a more traditional suit. The versatility of **Dege & Skinner** is great for special requests – from uniforms to tweeds, but if bold splashes of colour and innovative, fashion-led designs appeal, turn to the younger generation **Richard Anderson**, **Richard James** and **Ozwald Boateng**.

Suitable suits

Having a suit custom tailored for men is a unique experience, and not one that's necessarily limited to men from the upper echelons of society. Away from Savile Row (and Savile Row prices), City-based **King & Allen** offers a bespoke suit service for under £300, while **Mr Eddie** (now joined in his Soho premises by his son Chris Kerr) is the place to go for a natty suit with flamboyant flair. Think Johnny Depp chic – stylish, but with a certain *je ne sais quoi*. Fellow Soho-ite **John Pearse** is also a specialist in the eccentric stakes. That's not to say his salon is exclusively experimental, but if something quirky or classic-with-a-twist takes your fancy, hot foot it to his workshop.

The dedicated dandy should also consider **Timothy Everest**, whose bespoke service comes with the tagline "Always remember, you dress to fascinate others, not yourself." The atelier's premises in an 18th-century house in the East End are an idyllic foil to the experience.

For those who consider Mod-chic infinitely more desirable, travel south to Elephant & Castle to visit George Dyer at **Threadneedleman Bespoke Tailors**. Or if a woman's touch is what's needed, make a date at **Susannah Hall**'s Clerkenwell atelier, which works with both men and women and will even make office visits to time-starved workaholics.

Shirt perfection

Most suit tailors will also run up a shirt, but you can't beat the specialists in the field. The quality is second to none at Jermyn Street favourite, **Turnbull & Asser**, where the Egyptian cotton shirts are woven to unique specifications. It also offers a bespoke tie service for the ultimate in top-to-toe coordination.

Nearby, award-winning shirtmaker **Emma Willis** is singularly perfectionist in the way she designs shirts for individual customers. As well as focusing on details like buttons, stitching, lining and cuffs, she advises on

James Smith & Sons
53 New Oxford Street, WC1

the most suitable weight of cotton for each shirt, which can vary from voile, batiste or oxford, to cashmere and cotton, depending on the lifestyle of the client.

In the shadow of St Paul's Cathedral, **Thresher & Glenny** has held a royal warrant from every monarch, ever since George III issued the first one in 1783.

Well-heeled gents

`03`

What's a truly dapper suit without an impressive pair of spats, brogues or loafers? For sartorially particular gentlemen, the West End is home to a trio of incomparable excellence: **John Lobb**, **James Taylor & Son** and **Tricker's**. Their heritage, classic designs and international reputation speak for themselves. At Lobb, precisely contoured lasts in beech, maple or hornbeam are fashioned for each client and stored for a lifetime. Lobb and Taylor make women's shoes too; men-only Tricker's has a bespoke service and a ready-made line crafted in its Nottingham workshop.

Also worth investigating is **Tim Little**, on the King's Road, who makes toe-tappingly fabulous footwear for a host of famous faces from Robbie Williams to Rod Stewart. For something more Elton John-crossed-with-The Beatles, carve a path to custom utopia at **Anello & Davide** in Kensington.

Bespoke for women

Women who know exactly what they like should experiment with **Orhan Kaplanbasoglu**. This north London based Turkish tailor can replicate a favourite suit or dress as well as copying designs from the catwalk and magazines, which is a secret really worth knowing. **Atelier Alice Temperley**, in Notting Hill, can create the most sublimely sexy creations for a party, whether you want to flash your legs or your cleavage – or preserve your modesty.

Screen sirens of the 1950s are the inspiration for **Kate Starkey Couture**'s range of shirts for women, and her bespoke service (run from studios in the City) exudes glamour. For luxury coats, **Katherine Hooker**'s custom-made designs are a joy. The Chelsea seamstress ensures the finished product has the most flattering bust-waist-hip combination possible, banishing those nightmares of stretched fabric in some areas and less-than-snugness in others.

Cashmere is an indulgence in itself, but both **Belinda Robertson** and **Ballantyne** truly excel when it comes to taking this luxury to new heights. The latter's Bond Street branch offers 131 colourways, which can be specially altered for customers who are tall or petite (or any size in between).

For the generously endowed, Knightsbridge-based **Rigby & Peller** (*brassière* maker to the Queen) has the edge on catering to your shapely needs, whether it be smaller, fuller, sleeker, or curvier. It can also make underwear to do the job that hours in the gym cannot. For on-the-beach chic, try **Biondi** near Sloane Square. Its made-to-measure bikinis will help to eliminate stressful body self-consciousness.

03

Belle on heels

Many women cannot have enough shoes. And who can beat a bespoke pair of heels? If you're in search of something dainty and sparkly, perhaps with a heart-stoppingly vertiginous heel, **Jimmy Choo Couture**, in Knightsbridge, will cut and stitch the goods with effortless panache. Former Jimmy Choo designer **Beatrix Ong**, based in Primrose Hill, adds a personal touch to her shoes. She can print text on the soles, so memorable dates, phrases or whatever quote you fancy, can be stamped cheekily on your sole.

Kilburn Park duo **Shirley Sum** and **Cynthia Fortune Rainey** teasingly promise to indulge clients' footlust with their bespoke service, and their elegant, feminine designs are named for individual couture clients. Near Baker Street is **Caroline Groves**, whose whimsical style harks back to a bygone era. She is refreshingly open

James Lock & Co
6 St James's Street, SW1

to incorporating unusual leathers, frills, trims, feathers, buckles, jewels and specially commissioned images within her designs to ensure that her clients are walking works of art.

Accentuating accessories

Any woman with style will admit that accessories are key: the devil is in the detail. While not strictly custom made, Covent Garden shop **Elliot Rhodes** has an exhaustive selection of belts and buckles that you can mix and match at your fancy to create the perfect design. Handbag diva **Anya Hindmarch**, on Pont Street, makes Be A Bags: take a picture and have it printed onto material and crafted into a clutch, a make-up zip-up, a tote, or a wheelie suitcase, with coloured piping, detailing and lining of your choice. Classic Bond Street brand **Mulberry**, also makes bespoke bags, for carry-it-all-in-your-own-way glitz.

Sparkling jewellery

For sparkling adornment with clout, a wealth of Bond Street jewellers can create personally designed masterpieces. For elegant classics approach royal jewellers **Asprey**. For rock-chic, visit **Fiona Knapp**'s Notting Hill jewel box of a shop. Rings are her forte, and her designs are confident, unfussy and bright. For more ornamental designs with a Grecian influence, head for the house

Philip Treacy
69 Elizabeth Street, SW1

of East Ender **Ben Day** and commission a precious gem trinket. For an original design for a special occasion, make an appointment with Marylebone designer Anthony Power at **Cox and Power** and create an exquisite piece of fine jewellery that exudes opulent luxury.

Head-turning hats

For crowning glory, there's nothing like a hat. Milliners **Philip Treacy**, on elegant Elizabeth Street, and **Stephen Jones,** in Covent Garden, make bespoke pieces fit for a queen. From trilbies to headdresses, all are lavish creations that are works of art in themselves, and perfect for showing off at Ascot. Exciting, young milliners garnering support include Stephen Jones' protégée **Gina Foster** and Emily Birch's venture **Diva Blue**, based in Primrose Hill. The former does some beautifully understated floral designs as well as dramatic 1930s-inspired pieces. Emily Birch's cocktail hats exude Golden Age glamour and her colourful, vibrant designs for hairpieces guarantee to turn heads, at less astronomical prices.

Signature scents

The final touch for any occasion is scent. **Roja Dove** ensures that creating your own perfume is a theatrical, but precise, performance. He mixes signature perfumes from the highest-quality raw materials at his haute perfumerie. Fragrances come in a Baccarat

Swaine, Adeney, Brigg Ltd
54 St James's Street, SW1

crystal flacon – a Georges Chevalier 1930s design that is re-blown especially for bespoke clients. At **Ormonde Jayne**, Linda Pilkington makes perfumes and scented candles, using exotic oils from around the globe. In Notting Hill, **Miller Harris** nose Lyn Harris turns perfume making into a unique experience. Be sure to pop into the scent garden before visiting the fragrance library and laboratory, where she will concoct a unique tincture of aromatic distinction just for you.

03

Specialist boutiques

Alongside bespoke delights, London is a haven for specialist shops, from shooting sticks, hip flasks and riding gear at **Swaine**, **Adeney**, **Brigg** or attire for the country squire at **Cordings**, to umbrellas in all styles and colours at **James Smith**. For chic luggage in which to pack your newly bespoke wares, try **Tanner Krolle** or **Globe-Trotter**, whose past clients have included Sir Winston Churchill and Sir Edmund Hilary. For cigars there's **Davidoff**, while for a proper hat (no fancy feather headpieces here), there's simply nothing better than **James Lock & Co**. Unusual perfumes and scents abound at appropriately named **Les Senteurs** and **Floris** feels like the grande dame of great English scented products.

Tailored living

Anderson & Sheppard
32 Old Burlington St, W1
⊖ Piccadilly Circus
📞 020 7734 1420
anderson-sheppard.co.uk
⊕ 6-7/N9

Dege & Skinner
10 Savile Row, W1
⊖ Piccadilly Circus
📞 020 7287 2941
dege-skinner.co.uk
⊕ 6-7/N9

Gieves & Hawkes
1 Savile Row, W1
⊖ Piccadilly Circus
📞 020 7434 2001
gievesandhawkes.com
⊕ 6-7/N9

Henry Poole
15 Savile Row, W1
⊖ Piccadilly Circus
📞 020 7734 5985
henrypoole.com
⊕ 6-7/N9

Huntsman
11 Savile Row, W1
⊖ Piccadilly Circus
📞 020 7292 4730
h-huntsman.com
⊕ 6-7/N9

Kilgour
8 Savile Row, W1
⊖ Piccadilly Circus
📞 020 7734 6905
kilgour.eu
⊕ 6-7/N9

Ozwald Boateng
9 Vigo St, W1
⊖ Piccadilly Circus
📞 020 7437 0620
ozwaldboateng.co.uk
⊕ 6-7/N9

Richard Anderson
13 Savile Row, W1
⊖ Piccadilly Circus
📞 020 7734 0001
richardandersonltd.com
⊕ 6-7/N9

Richard James
29 Savile Row, W1
⊖ Piccadilly Circus
📞 020 7434 0605
richardjames.co.uk
⊕ 6-7/N9

Suitable suits

Aquascutum
100 Regent St, W1
⊖ Piccadilly Circus
📞 020 7675 8200
aquascutum.co.uk
⊕ 6-7/N9

**Couturiere
(men and women)**
33 Brook St, W1
⊖ Bond Street
📞 020 7493 1564
⊕ 6/L9

John Pearse
6 Meard St, W1
⊖ Tottenham Court Rd
📞 020 7434 0738
johnpearse.co.uk
⊕ 7/O9

King & Allen
Victoria House, Charlotte Terrace, N1
⊖ Angel
📞 0800 027 4430
kingandallen.co.uk
⊕ 3/S2

Mark Powell
12 Brewer St, W1
⊖ Piccadilly Circus
📞 020 7287 5498
markpowellbespoke.co.uk
⊕ 7/O9

Mr Eddie
52 Berwick St, W1
⊖ Oxford Circus
📞 020 7437 3727
eddiekerr.co.uk
⊕ 7/O8

New & Lingwood
53 Jermyn St, SW1
⊖ Green Park
☎ 020 7493 9621
newandlingwood.com
⊕ 11/N10

Susannah Hall
110 Clerkenwell Rd, EC1
⊖ Farringdon
☎ 020 7253 4055
susannahhall.co.uk
⊕ 8/T6

Threadneedleman Bespoke Tailors
187a Walworth Rd, SW17
⊖ Elephant & Castle
☎ 020 7701 9181
threadneedleman
tailors.co.uk
⊕ 16/V15

03

Oliver J Benjamin
8 Kingly St, W1
⊖ Oxford Circus
☎ 020 7734 3334
oliverjbenjamin.co.uk
⊕ 7/N9

Timothy Everest
32 Elder St, E1
⊖ Liverpool Street
☎ 020 7377 5770
timothyeverest.co.uk
⊕ 8/Z6

Tom Lutwyche
83 Berwick St, W1
⊖ Oxford Circus
☎ 020 7292 0640
lutwyche.co.uk
⊕ 7/O8

Shirt perfection

Budd
1-3 Piccadilly Arcade,
SW1
⊖ Green Park
☎ 020 7493 0139
⊕ 11/M11

Emmett London
380 King's Rd, SW3
⊖ Sloane Square
☎ 020 7351 7529
emmettshirts.co.uk
⊕ 14/H17

Thresher & Glenny
50 Gresham St, EC2
⊖ Bank
☎ 020 7606 7451
⊕ 8/V8

Emma Willis
66 Jermyn St, SW1
⊖ Green Park
☎ 020 7930 9980
emmawillis.com
⊕ 11/N10

Russell & Hodge
3 Windmill Street, W1
⊖ Goodge Street
☎ 020 7580 7655
russellandhodge.com
⊕ 7/O7

Turnbull & Asser
71 Jermyn St, SW1
⊖ Green Park
☎ 020 7808 3000
turnbullandasser.co.uk
⊕ 11/N10

Well-heeled gents

Anello & Davide
15 St Albans Grove, W8
⊖ High Street Kensington
℃ 020 7938 2255
handmadeshoes.co.uk
⊕ 9/E13

G. J. Cleverley & Co
13 Royal Arcade, W1
⊖ Green Park
℃ 020 7493 0443
gjcleverley.co.uk
⊕ 11/N10

James Taylor & Son
4 Paddington St, W1
⊖ Baker Street
℃ 020 7935 4149
taylormadeshoes.co.uk
⊕ 6/K6

John Lobb
88 Jermyn St, SW1
⊖ Green Park
℃ 020 7930 8089
johnlobb.com
⊕ 11/N10

Tim Little
560 King's Rd, SW6
⊖ Sloane Square
℃ 020 7736 1999
timlittle.com
⊕ 14/H17

Tricker's
67 Jermyn St, SW1
⊖ Green Park
℃ 020 7930 6395
trickers.co.uk
⊕ 11/N10

Bespoke for women

Atelier Alice Temperley
6-10 Colville Mews, W11
⊖ Notting Hill Gate
℃ 020 7229 7957
temperleylondon.com
⊕ 5/C8

Ballantyne
153a New Bond St, W1
⊖ Green Park
℃ 020 7495 6184
⊕ 6/M8

Belinda Robertson
4 West Halkin St, SW1
⊖ Knightsbridge
℃ 020 7235 0519
belindarobertson.com
⊕ 10/K13

Biondi
55 Old Church St, SW3
⊖ South Kensington
℃ 020 7349 0430
⊕ 13-14/G13

Kate Starkey Couture
124 Middlesex St, E1
⊖ Liverpool Street
℃ 020 7100 1330
katestarkeycouture.com
⊕ 8/Z7

Katherine Hooker
19 Ashburnham Rd,
SW10
⊖ Sloane Square
℃ 020 7352 5091
katherinehooker.com
⊕ Off map

Mark Powell
12 Brewer St, W1
⊖ Piccadilly Circus
℃ 020 7287 5498
markpowellbespoke.co.uk
⊕ 7/O9

Orhan Kaplanbasoglu
Unit 2/3,
1-7 Orsman Rd, N1
⊖ Old Street
℃ 07817 439619
⊕ 4/Y1

Rigby & Peller
2 Hans Rd, SW3
⊖ Knightsbridge
℃ 0845 076 5545
rigbyandpelller.com
⊕ 10/I13

Belle on heels

Beatrix Ong
117 Regents Park Rd, NW1
⊖ Chalk Farm
☏ 020 7449 0480
beatrixong.com
⊕ 6/K1

Caroline Groves
37 Chiltern St, W1
⊖ Baker Street
☏ 020 7935 2329
carolinegroves.co.uk
⊕ 6/K6

Georgina Goodman
12-14 Shepherd St, W1
⊖ Green Park
☏ 020 7499 8599
georginagoodman.com
⊕ 10/M11

Jimmy Choo Couture
32 Sloane St, SW1
⊖ Knightsbridge
☏ 020 7823 1051
jimmychoo.com
⊕ 14/J14

Selve
1st Floor, 93 Jermyn St, SW1
⊖ Green Park
☏ 020 7321 0200
selve.co.uk
⊕ 11/N10

Shirley Sum and Cynthia Fortune Rainey
1 Victoria Mews, NW6
⊖ Kilburn Park
☏ 07838244006
sumfortune.com
⊕ 5/C8

03

Accentuating accessories

Anya Hindmarch
15-17 Pont St, SW1
⊖ Sloane Square
☏ 020 7838 9177
anyahindmarch.com
⊕ 10/J13

Elliot Rhodes
79 Long Acre, WC2
⊖ Covent Garden
☏ 020 7379 8544
elliotrhodes.com
⊕ 7/Q9

Mulberry
41-42 New Bond St, W1
⊖ Bond Street
☏ 020 7491 3900
mulberry.com
⊕ 6/M8

Signature scents

Miller Harris
14 Needham Rd, W11
⊖ Notting Hill Gate
☏ 020 7221 1545
millerharris.com
⊕ 5/C8

Ormonde Jayne
Royal Arcade, W1
⊖ Piccadilly Circus
☏ 020 7499 1100
ormondejayne.com
⊕ 11/N10

Roja Dove
Urban Retreat,
Harrods, 87-135
Brompton Rd, SW1
Knightsbridge
020 7893 8797
rojadove.com
⊕ 10/I13

Sparkling jewellery

Asprey
169 New Bond St, W1
⊖ Bond Street
℃ 020 7493 6767
asprey.com
⊕ 6/M8

Cox and Power
35c Marylebone
High St, W1
⊖ Baker Street
℃ 020 7935 3530
coxandpower.com
⊕ 6/L6

The London Silver Vaults
53 Chancery Lane, WC2
⊖ Chancery Lane
℃ 020 7242 3844
thesilvervaults.com
⊕ 7/S7

Ben Day
18 Hanbury St, E1
⊖ Aldgate East
℃ 020 7247 9977
benday.co.uk
⊕ 8/Z6

Fiona Knapp
178a Westbourne
Grove, W11
⊖ Notting Hill Gate
℃ 020 7313 5941
fionaknapp.com
⊕ 5/C8

Rach.L
Intimates, 11 St John's
Wood High St, NW8
⊖ St John's Wood
℃ 020 7722 7058
rach-l.co.uk
⊕ 2/H3

Head-turning hats

Cozmo Jenks
21 New Quebec St, W1
⊖ Marble Arch
℃ 020 7258 0111
cozmojenks.co.uk
⊕ 6/J8

Gina Foster
℃ 020 7565 2211
ginafoster.co.uk

Rachel Trevor-Morgan
18 Crown Passage, SW1
⊖ Green Park
℃ 020 7839 8927
racheltrevormorgan.com
⊕ 11/N11

Diva Blue
5 Ainger Rd, NW3
⊖ Chalk Farm
℃ 07717 790067
divablue.co.uk
⊕ off map

Philip Treacy
69 Elizabeth St, SW1
⊖ Sloane Square
℃ 020 7824 8787
philiptreacy.co.uk
⊕ 14/L14

Stephen Jones
36 Great Queen St, WC2
⊖ Covent Garden
℃ 020 7242 0770
stephenjonesmillinery.
co.uk
⊕ 7/Q8

Specialist boutiques

Bates the Hatter
21a Jermyn St, SW1
Green Park
020 7734 2722
11/N10

Cordings
19-20 Piccadilly, W1
Piccadilly Circus
020 7734 0830
cordings.com
11/M11

Davidoff
35 St James's St, SW1
Green Park
020 7930 3079
11/N10

Dunhill
48 Jermyn St, SW1
Green Park
020 7838 8000
dunhill.com
11/N10

Floris
89 Jermyn St, SW1
Green Park
0845 702 3239
florislondon.com
11/N10

Globe-Trotter
54-55 Burlington
Arcade, W1
Green Park
020 7529 5950
globe-trotterltd.com
11/N10

James Lock & Co
6 St James's St, SW1
Green Park
020 7930 8874
lockhatters.co.uk
11/N10

James Smith
53 New Oxford St, WC1
Tottenham Court Rd
020 7836 4731
james-smith.co.uk
7/P7

L. Cornelissen and Son
105 Great Russell St, WC1
Charing Cross
020 7636 1045
cornelissen.com
7/Q7

Les Senteurs
71 Elizabeth St, SW1
Sloane Square
020 7730 2322
lessenteurs.com
14/L14

Swaine, Adeney, Brigg
54 St James's St, SW1
Green Park
020 7409 7277
swaineadeney.co.uk
11/N10

Tanner Krolle
5 Sloane St, SW1
Knightsbridge
020 7823 1688
tannerkrolle.com
14/K15

03

See page 9
to scan the
directory

FASHIONABLE CULTURE
AND SMART ART

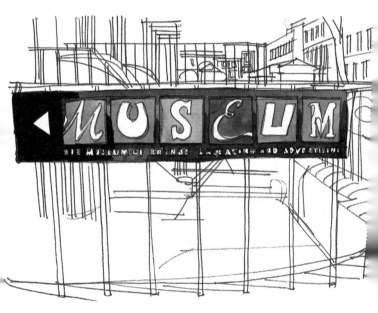

Fashion and Textile Museum
83 Bermondsey Street, SE1

Previous page: Somerset House
Strand, WC2

Londo celebrates to the hilt its wealth of historic heritage, but at the same time never shies away from embracing emerging cultural trends, the result is a unique melding of the old and the new. In this chapter we explore the capital's creative energy and pinpoint the most chic museums, most intimate galleries, and elegant homes in the most remarkable settings.

04

Fashionista chic

The **Victoria & Albert Museum** in South Kensington takes in an extraordinary breadth of decorative arts and design and is the leader when it comes to mainstream fashion exhibitions, having presented shows on such style icons as Vivienne Westwood, Italian *Vogue* eccentric Anna Piaggi and pop starlet Kylie Minogue.

For something more niche, visit Zandra Rhodes' **Fashion and Textile Museum**. The museum is the pet project of its founder, whose aim is to push fashion to the forefront of public consciousness as an art form and to make the vagaries of the industry more accessible to fashionistas and the uninitiated alike.

The **Museum of London** also houses an impressive array of sartorial delights, aiming to chronicle the city as a chameleon-like hub of fashion. From regal Tudor dresses to barely-there Mary Quant numbers, this is a dressing-up box worth rifling through for ideas.

Aesthetic indulgences

Some of London's most beautiful art collections are housed in buildings that are as stunning as their wares, and these are the places any self-respecting aesthete should visit. The **Wallace Collection**, displayed in Hertford House, the grandiose former residence of the Marquises of Hertford and Sir Richard Wallace, offers a breathtaking setting for paintings by Titian, Rembrandt, Velasquez and other works. Celebrated restaurateur Oliver Peyton has set up shop in the atrium and his restaurant is perfect for an atmospheric lunch.

Palatial **Somerset House**, once the public records office, is now home to the triumvirate of the Courtauld Institute, famed for its Impressionist paintings, the Hermitage Rooms with a changing display of precious items from the St Petersburg museum, and an eclectic array of silverware, mosaics and jewellery from the Gilbert Collection. Burlington House, another fine 18th-century building houses the **Royal Academy of Arts**, a chic rendezvous especially during the annual Summer Exhibition.

Houses and homes

Up in Hampstead, both Sigmund Freud's home, now the **Freud Museum**, and **Keats' House** are open to the public. Keats lived in this house for two years, falling in love and writing *Ode to a Nightingale* here, before travelling to Rome, where he died of tuberculosis.

For a less Romantic experience, seek out Freud's infamous couch, located in the house he fled to following the Nazi annexation of Austria in 1938. The library and study have been preserved just as he left them, and the rest of the house overflows with the antiques he amassed during his lifetime.

For the ultimate in house snooping, 18 Folgate Street has no rival. Pitched as a time-capsule extravaganza, **Dennis Severs' House** is a unique experience, a performance artwork that recreates the 18th-century aesthetic. This is no stand-behind-a-museum-rope affair – visitors wander round rooms that look as if the occupants have just left. The experience is most assuredly a sensory one, candlelit, with sounds and smells teasing at every turn.

In the former home of erudite early 19th-century architect **Sir John Soane**, the intimate and exclusive atmosphere attracts visitors as much as what is

04

The Serpentine Gallery
Kensington Gardens, W2

actually on display. Antiquities, curios, clocks and a fabulously eclectic selection of art, including works by Hogarth; treasures that should be sought out if you missed the humourist's 2007 exhibition at Tate Britain are highlights. Candlelit evening openings are held once a month. More recent art, notably Futurists, is on show at the **Estorick Collection of Modern Italian Art**, displayed in a fine Georgian house.

The **Geffrye Museum**, a homage to the middle class sitting room, is set up in a row of 18th-century almshouses. Each room is designed to reflect the sensibilities and style of a particular era, from 1600 to the present day via Georgian design, the opulence of the Victorians and the Art Deco chic of the 1930s. Outside, the period detail continues, with an immaculate herb garden and landscapes representative of the tastes of an assortment of eras.

04

Parks and gardens

On the chic fringes of Holland Park, the former home of Lord Leighton, now **Leighton House Museum**, is not so much a house as a wildly grand studio hung with pictures by John Everett Millais, Edward Burne-Jones and George Frederick Watts, as well as by Leighton himself. The Middle Eastern and European hybrid architecture is a fascinating feat of Victorian styling.

In contrast, for experimental artworks in simpler surroundings, visit the **Serpentine Gallery**, a heritage-listed tea pavilion in Kensington Gardens. This idyllic park location is best visited in summer, and indeed, the Serpentine Summer Party is one of the most exclusive events in the glitterati's London calendar. Mere mortals must be content with visiting its temporary exhibitions or enjoying various outdoor cultural and musical events, including cinema beneath the stars, when classic movies are screened for picnicking parties.

Further north, the rolling expanses of Hampstead Heath are home to statuesque **Kenwood House**, remarkable for its Robert Adam architecture and vast grounds, and a favourite for glamorous picnics during its open-air summer concert series.

Contemporary art

White Cube is the principal private gallery for cutting-edge culture. Run by Jay Jopling, husband of artist Sam Taylor Wood, the gallery has spaces in St James's and Hoxton that are favourites of the 'YBAs' (Young British Artists) – Tracey Emin, Damien Hirst, the Chapman brothers and Sarah Lucas, as well as emerging *enfants terribles.* **The Wapping Project** is a converted hydraulic power station that opened at the same time as that other converted power station, the

Tate Modern. This more intimate space leans toward the experimental and there's a fantastic industrial-chic restaurant, which sits adjacent to the now-defunct machines, perfect for pepping up fatigued minds and bodies.

Modern design

Across the Thames is the **Design Museum**, a Bauhaus-style feat of architecture. It is particularly worth visiting for the Designer of the Year exhibition, which always pinpoints interesting issues, and retains an intimacy and spontaneity that's often not found in larger gallery spaces. One off-the-beaten track museum that exhibits collections reflecting particular styles, trends and cultural influences is the **Museum of Brands,** collector Robert Opie's jaw-dropping assortment of otherwise unexceptional everyday items. They tell the story of our insatiable appetite for stuff, through a collection of artifacts from 200 years of unadulterated consumer indulgence, including advertising posters, mustard tins and biscuit packets.

04

Photography

For photography, definite must-visits are **Proud Camden**, **Proud Central** and the **Photographers' Gallery**. The latter was the UK's first independent gallery dedicated to photography. The **Michael Hoppen Gallery** is as much dedicated to selling as to viewing

White Cube
25-26 Mason's Yard, SW1

but its King's Road situation is perfect for a cultural interlude while on the shopping beat.

Private galleries

Cork Street, in Mayfair, and the labyrinth of streets peeling away from it, is a private gallery hub, and is a great nuclear base if you are thinking of buying. The atmosphere is smart and exclusive as of-the-moment names rub shoulders with the elite of London's gallery scene. For rock'n'roll chic, make time for **Scream**, an art gallery inspired by the wild ways of Rolling Stone Ronnie Wood. Detmar Blow's **Blow de la Barra** is another nearby gallery that provides a platform for interesting art, as do **Max Wigram**, **Haunch of Venison** and **Riflemaker**.

Further east, the art gets edgier but looses none of its punch. **Vilma Gold** heads up a concentration of ultra hip galleries around Bethnal Green, including the **Maureen Paley** gallery, the **Approach Tavern** (a pub with a gallery on the first floor), **Hales Gallery** (in the Tea Building at the bottom of Shoreditch High Street), **Dicksmith Gallery** and **Victoria Miro**, which make for a fabulously heady culture hit all in one go.

Fashionista chic

Fashion and Textile Museum
83 Bermondsey St, SE1
🚇 London Bridge
✆ 020 7407 8664
ftmlondon.org
✛ 12/Y12

Museum of London
150 London Wall, EC2
🚇 Barbican
✆ 0870 4443 852
museumoflondon.co.uk
✛ 8/W7

Victoria & Albert Museum
Cromwell Rd, SW7
🚇 South Kensington
✆ 020 7942 2000
vam.ac.uk
✛ 13/F14

Fashion Illustration Gallery
✆ 020 8543 67311
Fashionillustration
gallery.com

Royal Ceremonial Dress Collection
Kensington Palace, W8
🚇 High St Kensington
✆ 020 7937 9561
hrp.org.uk/
KensingtonPalace
✛ 9/E11

Whitespace Gallery
Vere St, W1
🚇 Oxford Street
✆ 020 7399 9571
whitespacegallery.co.uk
✛ 6/M8

Aesthetic indulgences

Dulwich Picture Gallery
Gallery Rd, Dulwich, SE21
🚉 North Dulwich
✆ 020 8693 5254
dulwichpicturegallery.
org.uk
✛ Off map

Royal Academy of Arts
Burlington House,
Piccadilly, W1
🚇 Green Park
✆ 020 7300 8000
royalacademy.org.uk
✛ 11/M11

V&A Museum of Childhood
Cambridge Heath Rd, E2
🚇 Bethnal Green
✆ 020 8983 5200
vam.ac.uk/moc
✛ Off map

The Foundling Museum
40 Brunswick Sq, WC1
🚇 Russell Square
✆ 020 7841 3600
foundlingmuseum.org.uk
✛ Off map

Somerset House
Strand, WC2
🚇 Temple
✆ 020 7848 2777
courtauld.ac.uk
✛ 11/Q10

The Wallace Collection
Hertford House,
Manchester Sq, W1
🚇 Bond Street
✆ 020 7563 9500
wallacecollection.org
✛ 6/K7

Houses and homes

Dennis Severs' House
18 Folgate St, E1
⊖ Liverpool Street
℃ 020 7247 4013
denissevershouse.co.uk
⊕ 8/Z6

Freud Museum
20 Maresfield Gdns,
NW3
⊖ Finchley Road
℃ 020 7435 2002
freud.org.uk
⊕ Off map

Keats' House
Keats Grove, NW3
⊖ Hampstead
℃ 020 7435 2062
cityoflondon.gov.
uk/keats
⊕ Off map

**Estorick Collection
of Modern Italian Art**
39a Canonbury Sq, N1
⊖ Highbury & Islington
℃ 020 7704 9522
estorickcollection.com
⊕ Off map

Geffrye Museum
136 Kingsland Rd, E2
⊖ Old Street
℃ 020 7739 9893
geffryemuseum.org.uk
⊕ 4/Z3

Sir John Soane Museum
13 Lincoln's Inn Fields,
WC2
⊖ Holborn
℃ 020 7405 2107
soane.org
⊕ 7/R7

04

Parks and gardens

Kenwood House
Hampstead Lane, NW3
⊖ Hampstead
℃ 020 8348 1286
english-heritage.org.
uk/kenwoodhouse
⊕ Off map

Marble Hill House
Richmond, TW1
⊖ Richmond
℃ 020 8892 5115
english-heritage.org.uk
⊕ Off map

Serpentine Gallery
Kensington Gdns, W2
⊖ Knightsbridge
℃ 020 7402 6075
serpentinegallery.org
⊕ 9/B13

**Leighton House
Museum**
12 Holland Park Rd, W14
⊖ High St Kensington
℃ 020 7602 3316
rbkc.gov.uk/
leightonhousemuseum
⊕ 9/B13

Open Air Theatre
Inner Circle, Regent's
Park, NW1
⊖ Regent's Park
℃ 0870 0601 811
openairtheatre.org
⊕ 2/K3

**Trafalgar Square
Festival**
Trafalgar Sq, SW1
⊖ Charing Cross
london.gov.uk/
trafalgarsquare
⊕ 11/P10

Contemporary art

Hayward Gallery
Southbank Centre,
Belvedere Rd, SE1
⊖ Waterloo
℃ 0871 663 2501
haywardgallery.org.uk
⊕ 11/S10

The Wapping Project
Wapping Hydraulic Power
Station, Wapping Wall, E1
⊖ Wapping
℃ 020 7680 2080
thewappingproject.com
⊕ Off map

White Cube
25-26 Mason's Yard, SW1
⊖ Green Park
℃ 020 7930 5373
whitecube.com
⊕ 11/N10

Modern design

David Gill
3 Loughborough St, SE11
⊖ Vauxhall
℃ 020 7793 1100
⊕ 15/S16

Design Museum
28 Shad Thames, SE1
⊖ London Bridge
℃ 0870 909 9009
designmuseum.org
⊕ 12/Z11

Museum of Brands
2 Colville Mews, W11
⊖ Notting Hill Gate
℃ 020 7908 0880
museumofbrands.com
⊕ 5/C8

Photography

Getty Images Gallery
46 Eastcastle St, W1
⊖ Oxford Circus
℃ 020 7291 5380
gettyimagesgallery.com
⊕ 7/N8

Michael Hoppen Gallery
3 Jubilee Pl, SW3
⊖ Sloane Square
℃ 020 7352 3649
michaelhoppengallery.org
⊕ 14/I16

Proud Central
5 Buckingham St, WC2
⊖ Charing Cross
℃ 020 7839 4942
proud.co.uk
⊕ 11/Q10

Hoopers Gallery
15 Clerkenwell Close, EC1
⊖ Farringdon
℃ 020 7490 3908
hoopersgallery.co.uk
⊕ 3/T5

The Photographers Gallery
5, 8 Great Newport St, WC2
⊖ Leicester Square
℃ 020 7831 1772
photonet.org.uk
⊕ 7/P9

Proud Camden
The Stables Market,
Chalk Farm Rd, NW1
⊖ Camden
℃ 020 7482 3867
proud.co.uk
⊕ Off map

Private galleries

The Approach Tavern
47 Approach Rd, E2
⊖ Bethnal Green
℃ 020 8980 2321
⊕ Off map

Blow de la Barra
35 Heddon St, W1
⊖ Piccadilly Circus
℃ 020 7734 7477
blowdelabarra.com
⊕ 6-7/N9

Dicksmith Gallery
74 Buttesland St, N1
⊖ Old Street
℃ 020 7253 0663
dicksmithgallery.co.uk
⊕ 11-16/Y14

Frith Street Gallery
59-60 Frith St, W1
⊖ Tottenham Court Rd
℃ 020 7494 1550
frithstreetgallery.com
⊕ 7/O8

Hales Gallery
7 Bethnal Green Rd, E1
⊖ Bethnal Green
℃ 020 7033 1938
halesgallery.com
⊕ 4/Z5

Haunch of Venison
6 Haunch of Venison
Yard, W1
⊖ Bond Street
℃ 020 7495 5050
haunchofvenison.com
⊕ 6/M8

Lisson Gallery
29 & 52 Bell St, NW1
⊖ Edgware Road
℃ 020 7724 2739
lissongallery.com
⊕ 6/H6

Maureen Paley
21 Herald St, E2
⊖ Bethnal Green
℃ 020 7729 4112
maureenpaley.com
⊕ Off map

Max Wigram
99 New Bond St, W1
⊖ Bond Street
℃ 020 7495 4960
maxwigram.com
⊕ 6/M8

Riflemaker
79 Beak St, W1
⊖ Piccadilly Circus
℃ 020 7439 0000
riflemaker.org
⊕ 6-7/N9

Sartorial Contemporary Art
101a Kensington Church
St, W8
⊖ High St Kensington
℃ 020 7792 5882
sartorialart.com
⊕ 9/D10

Scream
34 Bruton St, W1
⊖ Green Park
℃ 020 7493 7388
screamlondon.com
⊕ 6/M9

04

Timothy Taylor Gallery
21 Dering St, W1
⊖ Bond Street
℃ 020 7409 3344
timothytaylorgallery.com
⊕ 6/M8

Victoria Miro
16 Wharf Rd, N1
⊖ Old Street
℃ 020 7336 8109
victoria-miro.com
⊕ 4/V3

Vilma Gold
6 Minerva St, E2
⊖ Bethnal Green
℃ 020 7729 9888
vilmagold.com
⊕ Off map

See page 9
to scan the
directory

05

RESTAURANTS, CAFES
AND TEAROOMS

The Wolseley
160 Piccadilly, W1

Previous page: Andrew Edmunds
46 Lexington Street, W1

London's gourmet scene has undergone a remarkable renaissance in the last decade. Whether it is old, established restaurants being taken over and given a new lease of life, or new, gastronomically daring diners popping up in unexpected locations, London has firmly established itself on the international gourmet map by nurturing a wealth of chefs whose culinary prowess is matched by slick designer decor and service.

05

Decadent dining

For decadent dining in the company of a veritable who's who of celebrities from politicians to fashion designers, Christopher Corbin and Jeremy King have scored a hat trick with **The Wolseley**, **Le Caprice** and **The Ivy**; restaurants that perennially steal the limelight and achieve relentless plaudits. The food is unswervingly good, the atmosphere sparkling with excitement, the service unstuffy, and the staff beautifully groomed and attentive. Corbin and King's **St Alban** appears to be even more popular – a glamorous design, starry clientele and commendable food have made it one of the hottest tickets in town.

Equally glamorous diners are drawn to the various **Gordon Ramsay** restaurants scattered across town, from his headquarters in Chelsea across to Claridge's and on to his East London pub The Narrow, via Petrus, the Savoy Grill, Maze, The Connaught, Noisette and the Boxwood Café.

The fiery Scotsman continues to dominate the London scene, and quite rightly so; his food, and that of his protégées, is inventive yet unfussy, experimental yet never overwhelming and the elegance of the restaurants themselves invariably reflects the detail and dedication invested into each dish. Look out for The Warrington, his pub, that's adding zing to the steady Little Venice restaurant scene.

For unrivalled theatrics, there is no place quite like **Les Trois Garçons**. Here the dramatic, over-the-top decor is the attraction. Adorning every surface is a menagerie of wild creatures glittering with jewels. A tiara-crowned white tiger growls at the entrance, while impala, a giraffe and other glamorous beasts draped in pearls and rubies lurk in corners.

At the other end of the scale, the pared-down glamour of **Tom Aikens'** eponymous Chelsea restaurant ensures all eyes are on each dish – every one a daring fusion of flavours. Unusual combinations are par for the course, and the best way to enjoy these adventurous creations is to try the tasting menu – a veritable marathon – which guarantees to chime hitherto undiscovered tastebuds. Further east, a worthwhile experience is **St John**, where nose-to-tail eating guarantees a flourish of offal surprises. No bone is left unturned, so if it's a tripe terrine or bone marrow salad that excites, this should be your number one choice.

London has greatly improved its repertoire on the fish front. **Green's**, **Bentley's**, **Scott's** and **J. Sheekey** (an unmissable gem in the collection of Corbin and King) are the places to go for an unrivalled maritime feast. Richard Corrigan has injected gastronomic zeal into what was the ailing Bentley's – take a seat at the bar and order velvety Guinness, oysters and the devilishly dark soda bread.

05

Pan-Asian and fusion cuisine

Perhaps the most significant culinary influence on London in the last few years has been pan-Asian, seen in the meteoric rise of chic restaurants like **Zuma**, **Roka**, **Hakkasan**, **Yauatcha**, **Umu**, **Bam-Bou** and **E&O**, which dazzle with mouth-watering exuberance. Evening meals have the added bonus of legitimising a bold foray into the expansive exotic cocktail menus.

The Holly Bush
22 Holly Mount, NW3

Ling Ling, the bar at Hakkasan, shakes an especially good zingy lychee martini, E&O does a mean mango daiquiri and Roka's subterranean bar, Shochu, pulls out all the stops with a bespoke shochu (Japanese spirit) service. The food in these places speaks for itself: delicate, unintimidating cuisine that blends delights from Asia with finesse. Umu's contemporary interpretation of Kyoto dishes is a real find, every detail is a marvel, down to the water flown in from Japan for the cooking.

Intimate spaces

Long-established Italian restaurant **La Famiglia** draws discrete celebrities with its seasonal Tuscan cooking. With its series of little rooms, **Julie's Restaurant & Bar** is a favourite of Holland Park's bobos while **La Poule au Pot** and **Odette's** offer familiar, straightforward dishes in intimate surroundings. At each, there's a local following that adds to the warm and friendly ambience, yet the places still feel exclusive. **Andrew Edmunds** is a favourite for romantic meals, low-beamed, laissez-faire and always a good choice for those with eyes only for each other. Among a cluster of restaurants in Shepherd's Market in Mayfair, **Le Boudin Blanc** is another gem for dinners à deux. Its candlelit ambience is most conducive for wooing and the food is positively aphrodisiac.

05

Luxurious lunches

A popular lunchtime spot for the Mayfair crowd is **Cecconi's**. This chic destination has been revamped by Soho House maestro Nick Jones, with an alluring interior designed by Ilse Crawford. If you can't get a table, sit at the bar and sample the tapas-style *cicchetti*, washed down with prosecco. Jones' informal brasserie in Notting Hill, the **Electric Brasserie** is also fun for lunch – whirring with chatter and achingly hip yet casual diners. The adjoining cinema is an indulgent experience for escaping inclement weather. Back in the West End, a cluster of cool customers are hidden just off Bond Street in Lancashire Court: **Hush**, **Rocket** and **Mews of Mayfair** are all perfect grazing grounds for the Gucci-fatigued. Round the corner, Japanese fusion eatery **Nobu Berkeley**, American diner **Automat** and **The Square** also attract the high-heeled, highly groomed glitterati, and suited-and-booted elite.

For a slightly out-of-town adventure, **Petersham Nurseries** in Richmond is the place. Set in a potting shed-cum-conservatory, the café and teahouse complement the rambling nature of the nursery but don't be fooled, this is gastro-gardening at its most refined. If it's hot, sit outside among the blooming plants, greenhouses and fountains and enjoy the delicate seasonal feasts presented by chef-of-the-moment Skye Gyngell.

Glamorous pubs

The London pubs remain the life-force of the capital, and any trip to London would be incomplete without a visit. **The Eagle** in Farringdon was London's original gastro-pub and remains brilliantly buzzy with delicious food served from the open-plan kitchen; its fizzing, sizzling and flames are a theatrical appetiser in themselves. Hampstead's **Holly Bush** is also a hidden gem. Located amid a labyrinth of cobbled streets and crooked stairs, this picturesque Georgian brick pub is the place to head for in winter. Hot bison-grass vodka is a hit with the pre-Christmas crowd.

For left-of-field chic, **The Camel** in Bethnal Green is a highlight. Its decadent wallpaper by innovative designers Cole and Son, the flamingo-adorned toilets, elaborately flocked seating area and gilded bar make this anything but a fusty local.

Terence Conran's son Tom transformed **The Cow**, in west London, serving pub food downstairs and more elaborate meals upstairs, and together with **The Westbourne** on Westbourne Grove, the two are magnets for the beautiful people flitting round Notting Hill. In once antiques-filled Camden Passage, urban-rustic **The Elk in the Woods** attracts a relaxed young crowd that has livened up this part of Islington.

Baker & Spice
47 Denyer Street, SW3

Smart tearooms

The British are constantly teased about their obsession for tea, and for good reason; so a pause for tea and cake is de rigueur while in London. **The Wolseley** and **Sketch** are two places that do high-glamour teas. **Konditor & Cook**, **Baker & Spice**, the **Primrose Bakery** and **Hummingbird Bakery** stand out for their cakes. Beautifully decorated, they are pieces of art in their own right – coloured sugary treats that will put a smile on your face, even if you're feeling blue.

Maison Bertaux and **Patisserie Louis** are the grand dames of the café genre. Patisserie Louis, in Hampstead is a famed Hungarian establishment, where weekend queues tail back as people wait with expectant glee for their iced bun or chocolate cake. Old-fashioned Maison Bertaux is the place for film industry types – many a high-flying deal has been struck here between mouthfuls of *pain aux raisins.*

05

Maison Bertaux
28 Greek Street, W1

Decadent dining

Bentley's
11 Swallow St, W1
Picadilly Circus
020 7734 4756
bentleys.org
11/N10

Chez Bruce
2 Bellevue Rd, SW17
Clapham South
020 8672 0114
chezbruce.co.uk
Off map

Club Gascon
57 West Smithfield, EC1
Farringdon
020 7796 0600
clubgascon.com
8/U7

Gordon Ramsay
68 Royal Hospital Rd, SW3
Sloane Square
020 7352 4441
gordonramsay.com
14/J16

Green's
36 Duke St, SW1
Piccadilly Circus
020 7930 4566
greens.org.uk
6/L8

The Ivy
1 West St, WC2
Leicester Square
020 7836 4751
the-ivy.co.uk
7/P9

J. Sheekey
28 St Martin's Court, WC2
Leicester Square
020 7240 2565
j-sheekey.co.uk
7/P9

Le Caprice
Arlington House,
Arlington St, SW1
Green Park
020 7629 2239
le-caprice.co.uk
11/N10

Les Trois Garçons
1 Club Row, E1
Shoreditch
020 7613 1924
lestroisgarcons.com
4/Z5

Momo
25 Heddon St, W1
Piccadilly Circus
020 7434 4040
momoresto.com
6-7/N9

Scott's
20 Mount St, W1
Green Park
020 7495 7309
scotts-restaurant.com
10/K10

St Alban
4 Regent St, SW1
Piccadilly Circus
020 7499 8558
stalban.net
6-7/N9

St. John
26 St John St, EC1
Liverpool Street
020 7251 0848
stjohnrestaurant.com
4/T4

Tom Aikens
43 Elystan St, SW3
South Kensington
020 7584 2003
tomaikens.co.uk
14/I15

The Wolseley
160 Piccadilly, W1
Green Park
020 7499 6996
thewolseley.com
11/M11

05

Pan-Asian and fusion cooking

Bam-Bou
1 Percy St, W1
⊖ Tottenham Court Rd
℅ 020 7323 9130
bam-bou.co.uk
⊕ 7/O7

Hakkasan
8 Hanway Pl, W1
⊖ Tottenham Court Rd
℅ 020 7907 1888
⊕ 7/O7

Umu
14 Bruton Pl, W1
⊖ Bond Street
℅ 020 7499 8881
umurestaurant.com
⊕ 6/M9

Eight Over Eight
392 King's Rd, SW3
⊖ Sloane Square
℅ 020 7349 9934
rickerrestaurants.com
⊕ 14/H17

Ping Pong
45 Great Marlborough
St, W1
⊖ Oxford Circus
℅ 020 7851 6969
pingpongdimsum.com
⊕ 7/N8

Yauatcha
15 Broadwick St, W1
⊖ Oxford Circus
℅ 020 7494 8888
⊕ 7/O8

E&O
14 Blenheim Crescent, W11
⊖ Ladbroke Grove
℅ 020 7229 5454
⊕ 5/A8

Roka
37 Charlotte St, W1
⊖ Goodge Street
℅ 020 7580 6464
rokarestaurant.com
⊕ 7/N6

Zuma
5 Raphael St, SW7
⊖ Knightsbridge
℅ 020 7584 1010
zumarestaurant.com
⊕ 10/I12

Intimate spaces

Andrew Edmunds
46 Lexington St, W1
⊖ Oxford Circus
℅ 020 7437 5708
⊕ 7/O9

Bistrothèque
23 Wadeson St, E2
⊖ Bethnal Green
℅ 020 8983 7900
bistrotheque.com
⊕ Off map

La Famiglia
7 Langton Street, SW10
⊖ Fulham Broadway
℅ 020 7351 0761
lafamiglia.co.uk
⊕ Off map

Assaggi
39 Chepstow Place, W2
⊖ Notting Hill Gate
℅ 020 7792 5501
⊕ 5-9/D9

Julie's Restaurant & Bar
135 Portland Rd, W11
⊖ Holland Park
℅ 020 7229 8331
juliesrestaurant.com
⊕ 9/A10

La Poule au Pot
231 Ebury St, SW1
⊖ Sloane Square
℅ 020 7730 7763
⊕ 14/L14

Le Boudin Blanc
5 Trebeck St, W1
⊖ Green Park
(020 7499 3292
boudinblanc.co.uk
⊕ 10/M10

Moro
34 Exmouth Market, EC1
⊖ Farringdon
(020 7833 8336
moro.co.uk
⊕ 4/T5

Odette's
130 Regent's Park Rd, NW1
⊖ Chalk Farm
(020 7586 8569
vpmg.net
⊕ 6/K1

Luxurious lunches

Automat
33 Dover St, W1
⊖ Green Park
(020 7499 3033
automat-london.com
⊕ 11/M10

Electric Brasserie
191 Portobello Rd, W11
⊖ Ladbroke Grove
(020 7908 9696
electricbrasserie.com
⊕ 5/A6

Mews of Mayfair
10 Lancashire Court, W1
⊖ Bond Street
(020 7518 9388
mewsofmayfair.com
⊕ 6/M9

05

Cecconi's
5a Burlington Gdns, W1
⊖ Green Park
(020 7434 1500
cecconis.co.uk
⊕ 11/N10

Hush
8 Lancashire Court, W1
⊖ Bond Street
(020 7659 1500
hush.co.uk
⊕ 6/M9

Nobu Berkeley
15 Berkeley St, W1
⊖ Green Park
(020 7290 9222
noburestaurants.com
⊕ 11/M10

Petersham Nurseries
Church Lane, Petersham
Rd, Richmond
⊖ Richmond
(020 8940 5230
petershamnurseries.com
⊕ Off map

Rocket
4 Lancashire Court, W1
⊖ Bond Street
(020 7629 2889
rocketrestaurants.co.uk
⊕ 6/M9

The Square
6 Bruton St, W1
⊖ Green Park
(020 7495 7100
squarerestaurant.com
⊕ 6/M9

Glamorous pubs

The Anglesea Arms
35 Wingate Rd, W6
🚇 Ravenscourt Park
☎ 020 8749 1291
✛ Off map

The Eagle
159 Farringdon Rd, EC1
🚇 Farringdon
☎ 020 7837 1353
✛ 8/T6

The Ifield
59 Ifield Rd, SW10
🚇 Earl's Court
☎ 020 7351 4900
ifield.com
✛ 13/E17

The Camel
277 Globe Rd, E2
🚇 Bethnal Green
☎ 020 8983 9888
thecamele2.co.uk
✛ Off map

The Elk in the Woods
39 Camden Passage, N1
🚇 Angel
☎ 020 7226 3535
the-elk-in-the-wood.co.uk
✛ 4/U2

The Nag's Head
53 Kinnerton St, SW1
🚇 Knightsbridge
☎ 020 7235 1135
✛ 10/K12

The Charles Lamb
16 Elia St, N1
🚇 Angel
☎ 020 7837 5040
thecharleslampub.com
✛ 4/U3

The Engineer
65 Gloucester Ave, NW1
🚇 Chalk Farm
☎ 020 7722 0950
✛ 2/L1

The Pig's Ear
35 Old Church St, SW3
🚇 Sloane Square
☎ 020 7352 2908
thepigsear.co.uk
✛ 13/G16

The Cow
89 Westbourne Park Rd, W2
🚇 Westbourne Park
☎ 020 7221 0021
thecowlondon.co.uk
✛ 5/A7

The Holly Bush
22 Holly Mount, NW3
🚇 Hampstead
☎ 020 7435 2892
hollybushpub.com
✛ Off map

The Westbourne
101 Westbourne Park Villas, W2
🚇 Westbourne Park
☎ 020 7221 1332
thewestbourne.com
✛ 5/A7

Smart tearooms

Baker & Spice
47 Denyer St, SW3
⊖ Sloane Square
℃ 020 7589 4734
bakerandspice.com
⊕ 14/I14

Brown's Hotel
Albemarle St, W1
⊖ Green Park
℃ 020 7493 6020
brownshotel.com
⊕ 11/M10

Hummingbird Bakery
133 Portobello Rd, W11
⊖ Notting Hill Gate
℃ 020 7229 6446
hummingbirdbakery.com
⊕ 5/A6

Konditor & Cook
10 Stoney St, SE1
⊖ London Bridge
℃ 020 7407 5100
konditorandcook.com
⊕ 12/W11

Ladurée
Harrods, 87-135
Brompton Rd, SW1
⊖ Knightsbridge
℃ 020 3155 0111
⊕ 10/I13

Maison Bertaux
28 Greek St, W1
⊖ Leicester Square
℃ 020 7437 6007
⊕ 7/P8

Patisserie Louis
32 Heath St, NW3
⊖ Hampstead
℃ 020 7435 9908
⊕ Off map

Patisserie Valerie
17 Motcomb St, SW1
⊖ Knightsbridge
℃ 020 7254 6161
patisserievalerie.co.uk
⊕ 10/K13

Paul
29 Bedford St, WC2
⊖ Covent Garden
℃ 020 7836 5324
⊕ 7/Q9

Primrose Bakery
69 Gloucester Av, NW1
⊖ Chalk Farm
℃ 020 7483 4222
primerosebakery.org.uk
⊕ 2/L1

The Ritz
150 Piccadilly, W1
⊖ Green Park
℃ 020 7493 8181
theritzlondon.com
⊕ 11/M11

Sketch
9 Conduit St, W1
⊖ Oxford Circus
℃ 0870 777 4488
sketch.uk.com
⊕ 6/M9

05

See page 9
to scan the
directory

COCKTAILS AND MUSIC
AFTER DARK

Claridge's
Brook Street, W1

Previous page: Café Royal
68 Regent Street, W1

L ondon's huge size could make going out daunting but it isn't if you know where to go. The number of options on offer is unparalleled, from pre-dinner cocktails to private members' clubs via all-night dance venues and roller discos, London has it all.

Hotel bars

As cocktail hour stretches out seductively ahead, act with some no-nonsense decisiveness and head for a hotel bar – say, **The Lanesborough**, **The Dorchester**, **Dukes**, **Claridge's**, the **Long Bar** at the Sanderson Hotel, and the **Berkeley's Blue Bar** (in case you were interested, that's Lutyens blue a startlingly blue blue as favoured by Edwardian architect Edwin Lutyens). Perennially dusted with a sugar coating of glamorous types, who, holding martini glasses aloft, they can be guaranteed to set the perfect mood.

06

Cocktail bars

Away from the cosseted protection of the hotels, and clustered together in Covent Garden, an abundance of bars lovingly prepare tipples for every aficionado's delectation.

Cocktails with old-school panache can be found at **Christopher's**, where the traditional drinks menu is treated with due reverence. At the other end of the scale, fabulously inventive concoctions with seductive monikers are on offer at **Freud**, a sparse, industrial den hidden beneath an antiques shop on Shaftesbury Avenue. A blackboard announces the potions of the season.

Souk Medina tempts its recumbent clientele, lounging on sequined cushions near a hookah pipe, with drinks mixed with rose water and exotic Moroccan spices.

In Mayfair, things step up a notch. **Sketch** has a variety of bars, each with a subtle twist, and all of them completely eclipsed by the toilets. On the first floor, bejewelled booths in midnight black capture the unsuspecting in glittering spider webs. At the back of the venue, giant individually cocoon-encased washrooms stand higgledy-piggledy, ready for custom. An unexpected draw, but unexpected never was so *farouche*.

Umu, **Cocoon** and **Volstead**, are other nearby glitzy haunts, each lurking down alleys and tucked behind, beneath or beside some of the grandiose buildings that line Piccadilly, Regent Street and Bond Street. The latter gives a wink to the speakeasies of the 1920s, which flew in the face of Andrew Volstead, the killjoy

American legislator who banned the sale of alcoholic drinks in 1919. All three bars revel in their out-of-the-way exclusivity; the intimate, in-the-know *joie de vivre,* which prevails there adds to their flirtatious appeal.

One tucked – away delight is **Gordon's Wine Bar** that is nestled in a subterranean ex-sherry warehouse on the Embankment. The low-ceilinged, dimmly lit and forever-crammed medieval vaults are unbeatable in terms of atmosphere, and the array of wines, more than 80, impress. Meanwhile, **Apartment 195** on the King's Road, **Trailer Happiness** in Notting Hill and East Ender **Lounge Lover** all serve a great cocktail and draw in an edgier crowd – a little more hip and a little less posturing than in the West End.

06

Members bars and clubs

Mixing with the mainstream is not for everyone and for those who like their company hand-picked, there's an abundance of private members' clubs. **Soho House** and the **Groucho Club**, house a smattering of media types, from the worlds of advertising, publishing, film and journalism, as well as models, actresses and music industry figures. **Blacks** and **Two Brydges Place** are two nearby clubs with less high-powered, more literary but infinitely cooler clientele.

Drinks with action

When simply drinking fails to satisfy, chic Londoners have brought the art of multi-tasking to their watering holes.

Popping up across the city are bowling alleys and karaoke parlours. Far from being shrouded in a mantle of shameless kitsch, they play up to the stereotype, turning it on its head. The result is these places are now destinations *du jour*.

Bloomsbury Bowling and **All Star Lanes** have borrowed 1950s Americana and mixed it with the insatiable British appetite for alcohol to create a bowling-and-cocktails extravaganza. The former is much more tongue-in-cheek, with so-tawdry-it's-cool decor and a self-effacing atmosphere. All Star Lanes is more polished, with cheekily dressed staff who take their cue from Betty Page. A great tip is to hire the private room, with two lanes and a bar, perfect if bowling straight is not a top priority.

Roller Disco at Canvas in King's Cross is similarly swathed in retro cool. **Lucky Voice** has private group karaoke booths so you can limit performance embarrassment.

In winter, **ice rinks** spring up across the city – warm up afterwards with a glass of spicy mulled wine. In summer, open air concerts are the thing. Take a picnic and settle down in the dusky light of one of London's great parks and let an operatic voice wash over you. Sublime.

The Hospital, **Milk & Honey** and **Westbourne Studios** attract a younger, less well-heeled crowd – bursting with energy, enthusiasm and creativity. **Annabel's** continues to attract a post-party crowd, while the appeal of **The Union** hinges on something altogether calmer – no less chic, but with a less-pronounced fervour for going wild and dancing until the wee hours.

Jazz and live music

London secrets away a number of live music venues whose cachet goes beyond the events they host. For jazz and atmosphere, the famed **Ronnie Scott's** (with plush leather and brass stalls), the **Vortex**, the **Jazz Café** and the **606 Club**, an intimate basement club and restaurant, all draw a weird and wonderful clientele that is part of their appeal. Serving up a wide-ranging live programme, **Spitz**, **La Scala** – a converted cinema, containing bars, dance floors and concert hall – and gallery-cum-music venue **Cargo** welcome a more loyal, defiantly muso crowd. Convivial **The Luminaire** serves up eclectic music, while larger venues like **Koko**, **Bush Hall** and **Hammersmith Apollo** hold larger events for a more diverse audience. Less mainstream is the **100 Club**, a great little venue on Oxford Street, which also hosts swing nights for more dapper movers and shakers.

All Stars Lane
Victoria House,
Bloomsbury Place, WC1

Glamorous nightclubs

When it comes to taking the party on, **Mo*vida** and **Boujis** are the favourite picks of keen-to-be-seen celebrities – from blue blood to rock royalty, all the major players have been here, and done that.

Mahiki, **The Paper Club**, **Pigalle**, **The Cuckoo Club**, **Kitt's** and **Kabaret's Prophecy** pick up the slack from these clubs, and hold equal, if not more appeal, if only because they don't trumpet their status as much.

Unusual clubs

Left-of-field clubs are generally where the chic urban crowd can be found; those keen to be where it's at rather than following who's at it (at least supposedly). The gilded, mirrored Grill Room at **Café Royale** on Regent Street invites oh-so-ironic posing for London's edgy elite. Tuesday's 1940s night is all about sartorial polish, filling up your dance card and admiring the view. Less outré, perhaps, are **Cherry Jam** and the **Notting Hill Arts Club**, which have cultivated their own brand of west London chic, focusing on music, mingling, and a more chilled-out ambience.

Various roaming clubs (**The Modern Times**, **The Whoopee Club**) have taken the burlesque ball (mirrored, naturally) and run with it, creating fabulously

06

Gordon's Wine Bar
47 Villiers Street, WC2

over-the-top nights in praise of sleek couture, burlesque performances and a flair for drama. **Hedges and Butler**, a labyrinth of passages in old wine vaults is one venue to play host to these nights, while the **Boogaloo**, **Bistrotheque** and **Bethnal Green Working Men's Club** host independent cabaret evenings.

Late night dancing

There are always those who need to crank things up that bit further, and **Fabric**, **Egg** and **93 Feet East** are the best places to start looking for parties that'll last into tomorrow. In King's Cross, Egg is clubber's heaven. Stylish, funky and smart, it's a welcome antidote to the myriad of grimy dives pumping out ridiculously high bpm. Fabric, set in a renovated Victorian cold store space in Clerkenwell, has four gigantic dance floors and is where serious clubbers go to shake their booty. 93 Feet East is a labyrinth of bars, dance floors and clubrooms along with a terrace for high summer lounging. Edgy, party-loving Shoreditch locals make this the last stop of the evening.

06

Hotel bars

The Dorchester
Park Lane, W1
🚇 Hyde Park Corner
☏ 020 7629 8888
dorchestercollection.com
✛ 10/L10

Claridge's
Brook St, W1
🚇 Bond Street
☏ 020 7499 2210
claridges.co.uk
✛ 6/L9

The Lanesborough
1 Lanesborough Pl, SW1
🚇 Hyde Park Corner
☏ 020 7259 5599
starwoodhotels.com
✛ 10/L12

Blue Bar, The Berkeley
Wilton Pl, SW1
🚇 Knightsbridge
☏ 0 20 7235 6000
theberkeleyhotellondon.com
✛ 10/K12

Dukes Hotel
35 St James's Pl, SW1
🚇 Green Park
☏ 020 7491 4840
dukeshotel.com
✛ 11/N11

The Long Bar,
Sanderson Hotel
50 Berners St, W1
🚇 Tottenham Court Rd
☏ 020 7300 1400
sandersonlondon.com
✛ 7/N7

Cocktail bars

Apartment 195
195 King's Rd, SW3
🚇 Sloane Square
☏ 020 7351 5195
jamiesbars.co.uk/
apartment195

Cocoon
65 Regent St, W1
🚇 Piccadilly Circus
☏ 020 7494 7600
cocoon-restaurants.com
✛ 7/N9

Gordon's Wine Bar
47 Villiers St, WC2
🚇 Charing Cross
☏ 020 7930 1408
gordonswinebar.com
✛ 11/Q10

Christopher's
18 Wellington St, WC2
🚇 Covent Garden
☏ 020 7240 4222
christophersgrill.com
✛ 7/Q9

Freud
198 Shaftesbury Av, WC2
🚇 Piccadilly Circus
☏ 020 7240 9933
✛ 7/O9

Lounge Lover
1 Whitby St, E2
🚇 Shoreditch
☏ 020 7012 1234
loungelover.co.uk
✛ 4-8/Z5

Shochu Lounge
37 Charlotte St, W1
🚇 Tottenham Court Rd
☏ 020 7580 9666
shochulounge.com
✛ 7/N6

Souk Medina
1a Shorts Gdns, WC2
🚇 Covent Garden
☏ 020 7240 1796
soukrestaurant.co.uk
✛ 7/Q8

Umu
14 Bruton Pl, W1
🚇 Green Park
☏ 020 7499 8881
umurestaurant.com
✛ 6/M9

Sketch
9 Conduit St, W1
⊖ Oxford Circus
☎ 0870 777 4488
sketch.uk.com
⊕ 6/M9

Trailer Happiness
177 Portobello Rd, W11
⊖ Ladbroke Grove
☎ 020 7727 2700
trailerh.com
⊕ 5/A6

Volstead
9 Swallow St, W1
⊖ Piccadilly Circus
☎ 020 7287 1919
volstead.com
⊕ 11/N10

Members clubs and bars

Annabel's
44 Berkeley Sq, W1
⊖ Green Park
☎ 020 7629 1096
⊕ 11/M10

The Hospital
24 Endell St, WC2
⊖ Covent Garden
☎ 020 7170 9100
thehospital.co.uk
⊕ 7/Q8

Two Brydges Place
St Martins Lane, WC2
⊖ Oxford Circus
☎ 0871 5287898
⊕ 7/P9

Blacks
67 Dean St, W1
⊖ Tottenham Court Rd
☎ 0871 2231 855
⊕ 12/V11

Milk & Honey
61 Poland St, W1
⊖ Oxford Circus
☎ 020 7292 9949
milkny.com
⊕ 7/N8

The Union
50 Greek St, W1
⊖ Tottenham Court Rd
☎ 020 7734 4113
unionclub.co.uk
⊕ 7/P8

06

Groucho Club
42 Dean St, W1
⊖ Tottenham Court Rd
☎ 020 7439 4685
thegrouchoclub.com
⊕ 7/O8

Soho House
40 Greek St, W1
⊖ Leicester Square
☎ 020 7734 5188
sohohouse.com
⊕ 7/P8

Westbourne Studios
242 Acklam Rd, W10
⊖ Westbourne Park
☎ 020 7575 3000
westbournestudios.com
⊕ 5/B7

Drinks with action

All Star Lanes
Victoria House,
Bloomsbury Pl, WC1
⊖ Holborn
ⓒ 020 7025 2676
allstarlanes.co.uk
⊕ 7/Q7

Bloomsbury Bowling
Tavistock Hotel,
Bedford Way, WC1
⊖ Russell Square
ⓒ 020 7183 1979
bloomsburybowling.com
⊕ 3-7/P5

Clapham Common Outdoor Concerts
⊖ Clapham Common
ⓒ 020 7622 5745
claphamcommon.org.uk
⊕ Off map

The Comedy Store
1a Oxendon St, SW1
⊖ Piccadilly
ⓒ 0870 060 2340
thecomedystore.co.uk
⊕ 7/O9

Kenwood Outdoor Concerts
Hampstead Lane, NW6
⊖ Hampstead
ⓒ 020 8348 1286
english-heritage.org.uk/kenwoodhouse
⊕ Off map

Lucky Voice
52 Poland St, W1
⊖ Oxford Circus
ⓒ 020 7439 3660
luckyvoice.co.uk
⊕ 7/N8

Natural History Museum
(outdoor ice skating)
Cromwell Rd, SW7
⊖ South Kensington
ⓒ 020 7942 5000
nhm.ac.uk
⊕ 13/F14

Opera Holland Park
Box Office, Stable Yard, W8
⊖ Holland Park
ⓒ 0845 230 9769
rbkc.gov.uk/orphollandpark
⊕ 9/B12

Pétanque at Balls Brothers
Hay's Galleria,
Tooley St, SE1
⊖ London Bridge
ⓒ 020 7407 4301
ballsbrothers.co.uk
⊕ 12/Y12

Roller Disco at Canvas
King's Cross Freight
Depot, York Way, N1
⊖ King's Cross
rollerdisco.info
⊕ 3/Q3

Somerset House
(outdoor ice skating)
Strand, WC2
⊖ Temple
ⓒ 020 7845 4600
somerset-house.org.uk
⊕ 11/Q10

The Winery
(wine tastings)
Liberty, Great
Marlborough St, W1
⊖ Oxford Circus
ⓒ 020 7734 3239
thewineryuk.com
⊕ 7/N8

Jazz and live music

100 Club
100 Oxford St, W1
⊖ Oxford Circus
☏ 020 7636 0933
the100club.co.uk
⊕ 6/K8

The 606 Club
90 Lots Rd, SW10
⊖ Sloane Square
☏ 0871 3324 104
606club.co.uk
⊕ Off map

Bush Hall
310 Uxbridge Rd, W12
⊖ Shepherd's Bush
☏ 020 8222 6955
bushhallmusic.co.uk
⊕ Off map

Cargo
Kingsland Viaduct,
83 Rivington St, EC2
⊖ Shoreditch
☏ 020 7739 3440
cargo-london.com
⊕ 4-8/Y5

Hammersmith Apollo
Queen Caroline St, W6
⊖ Hammersmith
☏ 020 8563 3800
⊕ Off map

Jazz Café
5 Parkway, NW1
⊖ Camden
☏ 0871 0751 742
meanfiddler.com
⊕ 2/M1

Koko
1A Camden High St, NW1
⊖ Camden
☏ 0870 4325 527
koko.uk.com
⊕ 3/N1

La Scala
275 Pentonville Rd, N1
⊖ King's Cross
☏ 020 7833 2022
scala-london.co.uk
⊕ 3/R3

The Luminaire
311 Kilburn High Rd, NW6
⊖ Kilburn
☏ 020 7372 7123
theluminaire.co.uk
⊕ 1/D1

Pizza on the Park
11-13 Knightsbridge, SW1
⊖ Hyde Park Corner
☏ 020 7734 3220
pizzaexpresslive.co.uk
⊕ 10/J12

Proud Camden
The Stables Market,
Chalk Farm Rd, NW1
⊖ Camden
☏ 020 7482 3867
proud.co.uk
⊕ Off map

Proud Central
Buckingham St, WC2
⊖ Charing Cross
☏ 020 7839 4942
proud.co.uk
⊕ 11/Q10

Ronnie Scott's
47 Frith St, W1
⊖ Tottenham Court Rd
☏ 020 7439 0747
ronniescotts.co.uk
⊕ 7/O8

Spitz
109 Commercial St, E1
⊖ Liverpool Street
☏ 020 7392 9032
spitz.co.uk
⊕ 8/Z6

Vortex
11 Gillett St, N16
⊖ Highbury & Islington
☏ 020 7254 4097
vortexjazz.co.uk
⊕ Off map

06

Glamorous nightclubs

Boujis
43 Thurloe St, SW7
⊖ South Kensington
☏ 020 7584 2000
boujis.com
⊕ 14/H14

Kitts
7 Sloane Sq, SW1
⊖ Sloane Square
☏ 020 7881 5990
kitts-london.com
⊕ 14/K14

The Paper Club
68 Regent St, W1
⊖ Piccadilly Circus
☏ 020 7439 7770
⊕ 7/N9

Cuckoo Club
Swallow St, W1
⊖ Piccadilly Circus
☏ 020 7287 4300
thecuckooclub.com
⊕ 11/N10

Mahiki
1 Dover St, W1
⊖ Green Park
☏ 020 7493 9529
mahiki.com
⊕ 11/M10

Pigalle
215 Piccadilly, W1
⊖ Piccadilly Circus
☏ 020 7734 8142
vpmg.net/pigalle
⊕ 11/M11

Kabaret's Prophecy
16-18 Beak St, W1
⊖ Oxford Circus
☏ 020 7439 2229
kabaretsprophecy.com
⊕ 6-7/N9

Mo*vida
8-9 Argyll St, W1
⊖ Oxford Circus
☏ 020 7734 5776
movida-club.com
⊕ 7/N8

TwentyFour
24 Kingly St, W1
⊖ Oxford Circus
☏ 020 7494 9835
24london.eu
⊕ 7/N9

Unusual clubs

Bethnal Green Working Men's Club
44 Pollard Row, E2
⊖ Bethnal Green
☏ 020 7739 7170
workersplaytime.net
⊕ Off map

The Boogaloo
312 Archway Rd, N6
⊖ Highgate
☏ 020 8340 2928
theboogaloo.co.uk
⊕ Off map

Cherry Jam
58 Porchester Rd, W2
⊖ Bayswater
☏ 020 7727 9950
Cherryjam.net
⊕ 5/E7

Bistrotheque
23 Wadeson St, E2
⊖ Bethnal Green
☏ 020 8983 7900
bistrotheque.com
⊕ Off map

Café Royal
68 Regent St, W1
⊖ Piccadilly Circus
☏ 020 7437 9090
⊕ 7/N9

Dragon Bar
5 Leonard St, EC2
⊖ Old Street
☏ 020 7490 7110
⊕ 4-8/Y5

**Dream Bags
Jaguar Shoes**
32 Kingsland Rd, E2
⊖ Shoreditch
☏ 020 7739 9550
jaguarshoes.com
⊕ 4/Z3

Guanabara
Parker St, WC2
⊖ Covent Garden
☏ 020 7242 8600
guanabara.co.uk
⊕ 7/Q8

Hedges and Butler
153 Regent St, W1
⊖ Oxford Circus
☏ 020 7434 2232
hedgesandbutler.co.uk
⊕ 7/N9

Madame JoJo's
8 Brewer St, W1
⊖ Piccadilly Circus
☏ 020 7734 3040
madamejojos.com
⊕ 7/O9

The Modern Times
☏ 020 7734 0796
themoderntimesclub.
co.uk

Notting Hill Arts Club
21 Notting Hill Gate,
W11
⊖ Notting Hill Gate
☏ 020 7598 5226
nottinghillartsclub.com
⊕ 9/C10

The Roxy
3 Rathbone Pl, W1
⊖ Tottenham Court Rd
☏ 020 7225 1098
theroxy.co.uk
⊕ 7/O7

Vibe Bar
The Old Truman Brewery,
91 Brick Lane, E1
⊖ Shoreditch
☏ 020 7426 0491
vibe-bar.co.uk
⊕ Off map

The Whoopee Club
thewhoopeeclub.com

`06`

Late night dancing

93 Feet East
150 Brick Lane, E1
⊖ Shoreditch
☏ 020 7247 3293
93feeteast.co.uk
⊕ Off map

Egg
200 York Way, N7
⊖ King's Cross
☏ 020 7609 8364
egglondon.net
⊕ 3/Q1

Fabric
77a Charterhouse St, EC1
⊖ Farringdon
☏ 020 7336 8898
fabriclondon.com
⊕ 8/T7

See page 9
to scan the
directory

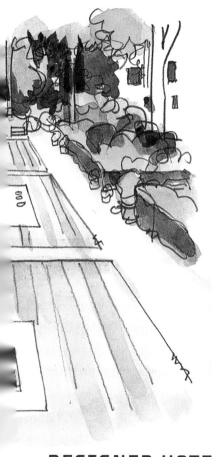

DESIGNER HOTELS
AND GUESTHOUSES

Previous page: The Hempel
31-35 Craven Hill Gardens, W2

The Ritz
150 Piccadilly, W1

S tylish, intimate, original and luxurious options for laying your head to rest after a hard day's shopping, working or partying are virtually limitless in London. Pick your accomodation perfectly, and every flight of fancy can be indulged.

Grand hotels

In spite of the Zeitgeist vacillations of the metropolis, London's hotel grandees, famed for their history, elegance, opulence and period glamour, retain their internationally renowned status, with nothing but tweaks to keep them at the top of their game (Bluetooth here, entertainment systems there, all discreetly installed so as not to disturb the Old World grandeur of their surroundings).

07

Leading the crowd is invariably **The Ritz**, its stately edifice a much-loved landmark superciliously looming over Piccadilly and Green Park, and its Italian garden is one of the most beautiful in Europe.

Claridge's, **Brown's Hotel**, **The Savoy** and **The Dorchester** complete the roster of London's regal hotel quintet. Claridge's wows from the start, with its chauffeured elevator, complete with a sofa. And if this mini adventure takes you to the Art Deco decadence of the Brook Suite, so much the better. Round the corner, Olga Polizzi and Sir Rocco Forte have injected Brown's with an understated elegance that breathes life into London's original luxury hotel.

Townhouse elegance

Townhouse chic is what London does best. With low-key nonchalance, the sumptuously intimate **Hazlitt's** lurks behind the facades of three houses on Frith Street, right in the bustling, pulsating heart of Soho. Wonky floorboards, imposing four-poster beds and dark wood panelling offset by rich colours, fabrics and designs, lend this haunt a quintessentially Soho feel – simultaneously louche, literary and luxurious.

The Lennox townhouse is on a leafy hideaway in Notting Hill, and celebrates its Englishness with something of a more colonial fervour (naval paintings, animal prints). **The Cadogan** in Chelsea is equally discreetly chic. The first of London's townhouse hotels, it is a late Victorian gem that makes no attempt at grand statements or over-designed precocity. Two garden suites lend an al fresco charm hard to match anywhere else in the capital. For something more theatrical, **Blakes**, the Anoushka Hempel designed Victorian townhouse swathed in lustrous, heavy fabrics and decorated with dramatic, fearless ornamentation, seduces with a heady, opulent allure.

An alternative is **The Rookery**. Named after the un-policed areas that quickly fell into disrepute in Dickensian London, this hotel is literally off the beaten track, a tricky-to-find series of houses in Smithfield, east London. Book the Rook's Nest, a fabulous suite with a ceiling that opens into a rooftop sitting room complete with breathtaking views over London.

Quirky boutique hotels

Hempel's in Notting Hill is an antipode to the drama of Blakes and an ode to all things minimalist. Thirty-two shades of white may seem unfeasible, but you'd better believe it. And don't be fooled into thinking this must make it bland. Suspended beds, others on platforms and impressive feats of masonry in the bathroom inspire anything but ennui.

07

Miller's Residence couldn't appeal to more divergent tastes; it's packed to the gills with curios, bric-a-brac and rare artifacts, which make for an intimate atmosphere celebrating 18th-century Romanticism. However, if you need to feel the full buzz of 21st-century London, **No.5 Cavendish Square** is ideal. The bars, restaurants, and roof spaces are used for parties

Great Eastern Hotel
40 Liverpool Street, EC1

for London's beautiful people, so you're guaranteed not to be far from the action for a millisecond.

Hip and artistic

The **Great Eastern Hotel** is another establishment whose halls are bursting with the wild ways of the glitterati both day and night. The former railway station hotel has seven bars and restaurants, not to mention a vast atrium, staircase and ballroom ripe for after-hours playtime – from hip book clubs via performance artists to costumed parties and impromptu catwalk shows, this is where it's at. The **Courthouse Kempinski** is another notable example of a hotel that has adapted considerably from its former uses. One-time 'residents' include Oscar Wilde and Napoleon – in the stocks. Wittily, the former magistrates court has converted its cells into bar booths, and the subterranean lair, which must at one stage have put the fear of god into London's lawless vagabonds, is now an über trendy spa.

07

The **Baglioni**, **Halkin** and **myhotels** in Bloomsbury and Chelsea easily rub shoulders in these style stakes. myhotel takes enormous trouble to make the hotel *your* hotel, with a personalised concierge service that caters for every whim. The Berkeley's rooftop pool, with its retractable roof, means the hotel effortlessly assumes an aura of cool. One less show-stopping feature, although no less fabulous, is the Prêt a Portea lounge. Fancy a Chloe bag in powder pink? Eat one decorated on a cake.

The whirlwind of chic London is perhaps best appreciated from the epicentre – hotels that are but a hop, skip and a jump from shops, culture, and nightlife. The Firmdale group (**Covent Garden Hotel**, **Soho Hotel**, **Charlotte Street Hotel**, **Knightsbridge Hotel**, **Number Sixteen**, **Pelham Hotel** and **Haymarket Hotel**) has seamlessly integrated itself into the way of life for cosmopolitan Londoners with the hotels' buzzy, chichi bars, private screening rooms and a eclectic clientele. Latest arrival, the Haymarket, even has a decent 18m pool and a five-bedroom townhouse available to rent. The hotels vary in size, but each retains a boutique vibe, mixing classic design, vibrant colour schemes and avant guard ostentation. It's worth seeking out the black and white room in the Soho Hotel; such monochrome splendour is a marvel.

Elsewhere, the Ian Schrager/Philippe Starck collaboration has stamped its mark on London with **St Martins Lane** and **The Sanderson**, both of which positively bubble over with fashionistas posturing and preening.

The edge is somewhat off the Light Bar, but The Sanderson's Long Bar still exudes nothing if not *Sex and the City* chic.

Cheap and chic

Alongside this glaring glamour, there has also been a renaissance of small hotels with affordable elegance. These cheap and chic gems, which include **base2stay**, **B&B Belgravia** and **Montagu Place** are intimate retreats that eschew the pomp and circumstance of larger hotels. Simple decor, centrally located, they have an unpretentious confidence that's winning.

Harlingford Hotel offers colourful boudoir style on a Bloomsbury crescent, while **Sumner Place** is an intimate minimalist haven. If knitted knickers are your thing, the **Weardowney Guesthouse** could be for you. The idiosyncratic hotel is run by celebrated knitting artists Amy Wear and Gail Downey, and their trendy boutique, Get Up, is on the ground floor.

07

The **Hoxton Hotel** is popular with business visitors to London because of its proximity to the City as well as to the buzzy, entertaining neighbourhood of Shoreditch. This is the perfect option for those on a flying visit who expect executive standards and personal service.

Weardowney Guesthouse
9a Ashbridge Street, NW8

Peace and quiet

Sometimes a break from the frenetic whirr is a welcome respite. **The Main House**, **The Mayflower** and Nick Jones' **High Road House** offer something for the world-weary traveller keen to escape for a moment's tranquillity. The good-sized apartments at The Mayflower provide an elegant home away from home and offer a real place to unwind. Caroline Main's west London bolthole is an airy sanctuary that operates with simple and professional care. For the ultimate retreat, take either the first or second floor suite, which each occupy an entire floor, and have an adjoining sitting room.

Members' club **High Road House**, in Chiswick, has either playpens or playrooms and while both are small, their no frills, no fuss, elegance is winning, plus they are stuffed to the gills with goodies from Cowshed the Notting Hill spa also owned by Jones.

In the Earl's Court area, **Twenty Nevern Square**, a plushly decorated red-brick Victorian townhouse, overlooks a peaceful garden square. Nearby, the garden suites at the small, luxurious **Rockwell Hotel** have their own private garden terrace, perfect for a bit of outdoor peace and quiet.

07

Price indications are for a double room: £ up to £150; ££ from £151 to £250; £££ from £251 to £350; ££££ from £351 and over.

Grand hotels

Browns Hotel ££££
Albemarle St, W1
⊖ Green Park
(020 7493 6020
brownshotel.com
⊕ 10/M10

The Dorchester ££££
Park Lane, W1
⊖ Hyde Park Corner
(020 7629 8888
thedorchester.com
⊕ 10/K10

The Ritz ££££
150 Piccadilly W1
⊖ Green Park
(020 7493 8181
theritzlondon.com
⊕ 10/M11

Claridge's ££££
Brook St, W1
⊖ Bond Street
(020 7629 8860
claridges.co.uk
⊕ 6/L9

The Lanesborough ££££
Hyde Park Corner, W1
⊖ Hyde Park Corner
(020 7259 5599
starwoodhotels.com
⊕ 10/K12

The Savoy £££
Strand, WC2
⊖ Charing Cross
(020 7836 4343
fairmont.com/savoy
⊕ 11/Q10

Townhouse elegance

Blakes £££
33 Roland Gdns, SW3
⊖ South Kensington
(020 7370 6701
blakeshotels.com
⊕ 13/F15

Cranley Gardens Hotel £
8 Cranley Gdns, SW7
⊖ South Kensington
(020 7373 3232
cranleygardenshotel.com
⊕ 13/F15

The Lennox £
34 Pembridge Gdns, W2
⊖ Notting Hill Gate
(020 7229 9977
thelennox.com
⊕ 5/C9

Cadogan £££
75 Sloane St, SW1
⊖ Sloane Square
(020 7235 7141
cadogan.com
⊕ 14/J14

Hazlitt's ££
6 Frith St, W1
⊖ Tottenham Court Rd
(020 7434 1771
hazlittshotel.com
⊕ 7/O8

The Rookery ££
Cowcross St, EC1
⊖ Farringdon
(020 7336 0931
rookery-hotel.co.uk
⊕ 8/U6

Quirky boutique hotels

The Hempel ££
31 Craven Hill Gdns, W2
🚇 Lancaster Gate
📞 020 7298 9000
the-hempel.co.uk
✛ 5/F9

Malmaison ££
18 Charterhouse Sq, EC1
🚇 Farringdon
📞 020 7012 3700
malmaison-london.com
✛ 8/T7

The Mandeville £££
8 Mandeville Pl, W1
🚇 Bond Street
📞 020 7935 5599
mandeville.co.uk
✛ 6/L7

Miller's Residence ££
111a Westbourne Grove, W2
🚇 Notting Hill Gate
📞 020 7243 1024
millersuk.com
✛ 5/C8

No 5 Cavendish Square ££
5 Cavendish Sq, W1
🚇 Bond Street
📞 020 7079 5000
no5ltd.com
✛ 6/M7

Portobello Hotel ££
22 Stanley Gdns, W11
🚇 Notting Hill Gate
📞 020 7727 2777
portobello-hotel.co.uk
✛ 5/B9

Peace and quiet

The Berkeley ££££
Wilton Pl, SW1
🚇 Knightsbridge
📞 0 20 7235 6000
theberkeleyhotellondon.com
✛ 10/K12

Bingham ££
61-63 Petersham Rd,
Richmond
🚇 Richmond
📞 020 8940 0902
binghamhotel.co.uk
✛ Off map

Draycott Hotel £££
26 Cadogan Gdns, SW3
🚇 Sloane Square
📞 draycotthotel.com
✛ 14/J14

High Road House ££
162 Chiswick High Rd, W4
🚇 Turnham Green
📞 020 8742 1717
highroadhouse.co.uk
✛ Off map

The Main House £
6 Colville Rd, W11
🚇 Notting Hill Gate
📞 020 7221 9691
themainhouse.com
✛ 5/C9

The Mayflower £
26-28 Trebovir Rd, SW5
🚇 Earl's Court
📞 020 7370 0991
mayflowerhotel.co.uk
✛ 13/C15

The Montague £££
15 Montague St, WC1
🚇 Russell Square
📞 020 7637 1001
montaguehotel.com
✛ 7/Q6

The Rockwell ££
181 Cromwell Rd, SW5
🚇 Earl's Court
📞 020 7244 2000
therockwellhotel.com
✛ 13/F14

Twenty Nevern Square ££
20 Nevern Sq, SW5
🚇 Earl's Court
📞 020 7565 9555
twentynevernsquare.co.uk
✛ 13/C15

07

Urban buzz

Charlotte Street Hotel £££
15-17 Charlotte St, W1
🚇 Tottenham Court Rd
℅ 020 7806 2000
firmdale.com
✪ 7/N6

No.5 Maddox St £££
5 Maddox St, W1
🚇 Oxford Circus
℅ 020 7647 0200
living-rooms.co.uk
✪ 6/M9

The Sanderson ££
50 Berners St, W1
🚇 Tottenham Court Rd
℅ 020 7300 1400
sandersonlondon.com
✪ 7/N7

Covent Garden Hotel £££
10 Monmouth St, WC2
🚇 Covent Garden
℅ 020 7806 1000
firmdale.com
✪ 7/P8

Number Sixteen ££
16 Sumner Pl, SW7
🚇 South Kensington
℅ 020 7589 5232
firmdale.com
✪ 13-14/G15

The Soho Hotel £££
4 Richmond Mews, W1
🚇 Tottenham Court Rd
℅ 020 7559 3000
firmdale.com
✪ 7/O8

Haymarket Hotel £££
1 Suffolk Pl, SW1
🚇 Piccadilly Circus
℅ 020 7470 4000
firmdale.co.uk
✪ 11/P10

One Aldwych ££££
1 Aldwych, WC2
🚇 Temple
℅ 020 7300 1000
onealdwych.com
✪ 7/R9

St Martins Lane Hotel £££
45 St Martin's Lane, WC2
🚇 Oxford Circus
℅ 020 7300 5500
stmartinslane.com
✪ 7/P9

Knightsbridge Hotel ££
10 Beaufort Gdns, SW3
🚇 Knightsbridge
℅ 020 7584 6300
firmdale.com
✪ 10/I13

The Pelham Hotel ££
15 Cromwell Pl, SW7
🚇 South Kensington
℅ 020 7589 8288
firmdale.com
✪ 13/G14

The Trafalgar £££
2 Spring Gdns, SW1
🚇 Charing Cross
℅ 020 7870 2900
thetrafalgar.com
✪ 11/P10

Cheap and chic

B&B Belgravia £
64 Ebury St, SW1
🚇 Victoria
℅ 020 7259 8570
bb-belgravia.com
✪ 10/L14

Harlingford Hotel £
61 Cartwright Gdns, WC1
🚇 Russell Square
℅ 020 7387 1551
harlingfordhotel.com
✪ 3/P4

**Premier Travel Inn
London County Hall** £
Belvedere Rd, SE1
🚇 Waterloo
℅ 0870 238 3300
premiertravelinn.com
✪ 11/R11

base2stay £
25 Courtfield Gdns, SW5
◉ Earl's Court
(020 7244 2255
base2stay.com
◉ 13/E15

Hoxton Hotel £
81 Great Eastern St, EC2
◉ Old Street
(020 7550 1000
hoxtonhotels.com
◉ 4/Y5

Sumner Place £
54 Upper Berkeley St, W1
◉ Marble Arch
(020 7723 2244
thesumner.com
◉ 6/J8

Guesthouse West £
163 Westbourne Grove, W11
◉ Notting Hill Gate
(020 7792 9800
guesthousewest.com
◉ 5/C8

Montagu Place ££
2 Montagu Pl, W1
◉ Baker Street
(020 7467 2777
montagu-place.co.uk
◉ 7/Q6

**Weardowney
Guesthouse** £
9a Ashbridge St, NW8
◉ Marylebone
(020 7725 9694
weardowney.com
◉ 2/H5

Hip and artistic

Baglioni £££
60 Hyde Park Gate, SW7
◉ Hyde Park Corner
(020 7368 5700
baglionihotels.com
◉ 9/F12

Great Eastern Hotel ££££
40 Liverpool St, EC1
◉ Liverpool Street
(020 7618 5000
great-eastern-hotel.co.uk
◉ 8/Y7

myhotel Bloomsbury ££
11 Bayley St, WC1
◉ Tottenham Court Rd
(020 7667 6000
myhotels.co.uk
◉ 7/O7

07

Courthouse Kempinski £££
19 Gt Marlborough St, W1
◉ Oxford Street
(020 7297 5555
courthouse-hotel.com
◉ 7/N8

Halkin ££££
5 Halkin St, SW1
◉ Victoria
(020 7333 1000
halkin.como.bz
◉ 10/L12

myhotel Chelsea ££
35 Ixworth Pl, SW3
◉ South Kensington
(020 7225 7500
myhotels.co.uk
◉ 14/H15

See page 9 to scan the directory

08

SPAS, GROOMING AND RELAXATION

Spa Illuminata
63 South Audley Street, W1

Previous page: The Hurlingham Club
Ranelagh Gardens, SW6

The über activity inherent in a trip to London can be overwhelming. With long distances to traverse between the cultural delights, sartorial havens and gastronomic extravaganzas, it can be hard to find the time for plain old rest and relaxation. Step forward to London's top groomers, pamperers and blissful spa providers.

Top-drawer pampering

Elemis, **Bliss**, **Spa Illuminata** and **Cowshed** are the top independent spas for pampering. For an instantaneous wind down, visit Spa Illuminata's steam room, before indulging in some of the treatments. Holland Park's Cowshed is perfectly compact, but offers a wealth of relaxing and grooming options – the maintenance pedicure and facial combination is particularly good. Two therapists work on you at the same time, buffing and polishing intently for pristine results.

For an excellent facial, visit the **Eve Lom Clinic** – the internationally renowned cleansing specialist's products speak volumes, but for the real deal, a personal visit is a must. The rosemary and mint awakening body wrap at the **Aveda Spa** in Covent Garden is essential for those

08

in need of a pick-me-up. And for essential grooming on the go, try **Urban Retreat** at Harrods, which promises dedication to 'replenishing the modern luxuries of time, space and comfort'. **Spa.NK**, like the Space.NK apothecary, gathers findings from around the globe for the ultimate in relaxation. Try its signature massage, or the urban detox, which combines the healing benefits of ayurvedic lymphatic drainage and thermotherapy techniques to stimulate and purify. For holistic beauty treatments, test out the **Organic Pharmacy**.

A number of hotels also have excellent spas. Among the best are the **Agua Bathhouse Spa** at The Sanderson, the **Mayfair Spa** at the Radisson Edwardian, **The Spa at Brown's Hotel** and the spa at the **Mandarin Oriental**, where treatments include its signature energy-restoring, shiatsu-inspired ginger ritual. All centrally located, they are nothing if not a welcome respite from the fractious *mêlée* of city life, and are open to hotel guests and visitors alike.

Talk-of-the-town grooming

Beauty may only be skin deep, but it pays to look resplendent, despite the time-consuming nature of top to toe grooming. To make it more of a treat than a chore, Topshop has installed a **Blowdry Bar** in its Oxford Circus headquarters. No booking is required, so you may have to wait, but at least there's ample retail distraction to keep you occupied.

The big names in hairdressing – **Nicky Clarke**, **John Frieda**, and the like – take reservations months in advance, but there are equally good bets including **Lockonego** – a chilled out Chelsea salon where you can have a cut while sampling some of the Asian-inspired snacks from next door restaurant **Eight Over Eight**. Or **Hugh & Stephen**, whose founder, Hugh Green, cuts the Duchess of Cornwall's hair and even did her hair for her wedding to Prince Charles.

Fashion-forward **Real Hair** has an edginess provided by stylists Belle Cannan and Josh Wood – hair grooming favourites at the runway shows of avant-garde designers. For colour, undoubted top dog is the Mayfair salon of **Jo Hansford**.

08

For top-to-toe grooming, London is home to some unrivalled specialists. **Otylia Roberts** is the waxing queen, but waxing bar **Strip** and **Body & Soul** are close competitors. The latter also offers electrolysis. **Xfolia** does laser treatments, and provides excellent consultations on pigmentation removal and other irksome body imperfections. Celebrated facialist **Vaishaly Patel** is also something

Geo. F. Trumper
9 Curzon Street, W1

of a whiz with thread, should that be your preferred method of hair removal. For nail treatments, **The Nail Lounge** and **Nails Inc** both make it their business to know what's hot and what's not. For specialist attention for your feet, visit **Margaret Dabbs**, or **Footopia** inside Peter Jones department store on Sloane Square. Many treatments at the latter are mixed on the spot; perfect for putting a fragrant spring in your step.

Gentlemen's hour

For that unique male pampering experience, some salons will ensure you come up smelling of roses. **Gentlemen's Tonic** is the perfect escape for those dallying about in Mayfair. It harks back to a bygone era but has modern quirks, like an individual LCD and sound system in each of the private booths, and sublimely polite staff, who do things the old-fashioned way.

For modern dandies, **Murdock London**, in the East End, caters for the new old-school man, who reads *The Chap Magazine* and ponders the acceptability of wearing brown in town. Traditional gentleman's barbers **Geo. F. Trumper**, with its mahogany-panelled private cubicles, and **Truefitt & Hill** are masters of the classic wet shave much appreciated by those who have no time for fuss or frills but like a job done properly.

08

Hampstead Bathing Ponds
Hampstead Heath, NW3

Gyms and health clubs

Pounding the treadmill is sometimes the best way to relieve stress, but only if it's in supremely aesthetic surroundings such as those at the super smart **Hurlingham Club**. Tennis, croquet and cricket are as much the form here as gym workouts. Personal trainer **Matt Roberts** should be able to show you the way to physical enlightenment, but if you'd like to get on with your workout unaided, check out the **Third Space**, **Lambton Place** and **KXGym** – three of the top gyms that offer a rather luxurious approach to exercise.

146

Centrally located, the Third Space has an oxygenated pool (as opposed to chlorinated) and an in-house DJ who plays tunes while you work out. It also has a high-altitude workout room in which budding explorers can train and offers some of the best classes in the city – highlights include burlesque, pole dancing and a yoga-dance fusion class.

Lambton Place is the haunt of Notting Hill's *jeunesse dorée*; one sublimely relaxing experience is to take a swim in the pool at night when the waters are mood lit. KXGym has a spa attached to the gym and the gym caters as much to hard-core workouts as to the relaxation and recuperation afterwards. A session in the martial arts studio can be followed by a massage or spell in the chill-out room.

For an exercise-cum-nightclubbing workout, descend into **GymBox**, the glamorous gym beneath St Martins Lane Hotel. If what you'd really rather do to let off steam aerobically is dance, arrange for a personal hip hop, jazz or funk lesson at **Pineapple Dance Studios** or **Danceworks**. If jiving is more up your street, stop in at the **100 Club** on Oxford Street for Lindy hop lessons, jive's wild sibling. Dress up, take a class and when that's over, dance to the live band all night – it's one form of exercise at any rate.

08

Inner peace

For something more Zen, **Triyoga** in Primrose Hill has ashtanga, iyengar and yin yoga classes, as well as Pilates classes; its dedication to holistic health is unquestionable. **Portobello Yoga**'s Zen Lunch, a lunchtime session aiming to rejuvenate, is also a class to mainline.

A simple swim is equally calming. London is scattered with lidos, but the **Serpentine** lake in Hyde Park is certainly the most stylish. For the most beautiful escape, wander across Hampstead Heath to any of the three **Hampstead Bathing Ponds**. Avoid the crowds on blistering hot days by aiming for early morning or late evening dips in these idyllic waters, surrounded by foliage. Swimming here in virtual solitude is one of the city's most enjoyable pastimes.

York Hall Baths and **Porchester Baths** are two of the better Turkish baths in London, and the latter also has Art Deco style Russian steam rooms, Turkish hot rooms and a Finnish log sauna, for a fully cross-continental experience. For an existential Sultan experience, the Turkish baths at the members' only **Royal Automobile Club** have no competitor. Flit between the 20°C in the frigidarium to 80°C in the laconicum for a committed cleansing process.

Top drawer pampering

Agua Bathhouse Spa
Sanderson Hotel,
50 Berners St, W1
⊖ Oxford Circus
℃ 020 7300 1414
sandersonlondon.com
⊕ 7/N7

Aveda Spa
The Aveda Institute,
174 High Holborn, WC1
⊖ Holborn
℃ 020 7759 7355
aveda.com
⊕ 7/S7

Bliss
60 Sloane Ave, SW3
⊖ Sloane Square
℃ 020 7584 3888
blisslondon.co.uk
⊕ 14/I15

Bliss Clinic
333 Portobello Rd, W10
⊖ Ladbroke Grove
℃ 020 8969 3331
bliss.me.uk
⊕ 5/A6

Cowshed
119 Portland Rd, W11
⊖ Holland Park
℃ 020 7078 1944
cowshedclarendoncross.
com
⊕ 9/A10

Elemis
2 Lancashire Court, W1
⊖ Bond Street
℃ 020 8909 5060
elemis.com
⊕ 6/M9

Eve Lom Clinic
2 Spanish Pl W1
⊖ Bond Street
℃ 0207935 9988
evelom.co.uk
⊕ 6/K7

Mandarin Oriental
66 Knightsbridge, SW1
⊖ Knightsbridge
℃ 020 7235 2000
mandarinoriental.co.uk
⊕ 10/J12

Mayfair Spa
Radisson Edwardian Hotel,
Stratton St, W1
⊖ Green Park
℃ 020 7915 2826
radissonedwardian.com
⊕ 10/M10

The Organic Pharmacy
396 King's Rd, SW10
⊖ Sloane Square
℃ 020 7351 2232
theorganicpharmacy.com
⊕ 14/K14

Shengaia
2 Erskine Rd, NW1
⊖ Chalk Farm
℃ 020 7722 2838
shengaia.com
⊕ Off map

The Spa at Brown's Hotel
Albemarle St, W1
⊖ Green Park
℃ 020 7518 4009
brownshotel.com
⊕ 10/M10

Spa Illuminata
63 South Audley St, W1
⊖ Bond Street
℃ 020 7499 7777
spailluminata.co.uk
⊕ 10/L10

Spa.Nk
127 Westbourne Grove, W11
⊖ Notting Hill Gate
℃ 020 7727 8002
spacenk.com
⊕ 5/C8

Urban Retreat
Harrods, 87-135
Brompton Rd, SW1
⊖ Knightsbridge
℃ 020 7893 8333
urbanretreat.co.uk
⊕ 10/I13

08

Talk-of-the-town grooming

Arezoo Kaviani
Hans Crescent, SW1
Knightsbridge
☎ 020 7584 6868
arezoo.co.uk
✇ 10/J13

Blowdry Bar
Topshop, Oxford Circus, W1
⊖ Oxford Circus
☎ 020 7636 7700
topshop.com
✇ 7/N8

Body & Soul
98 Cochrane St, NW8
⊖ St John's Wood
☎ 020 7722 8086
bodyandsoul-health.co.uk
✇ 2/H2

Cosmetics à la Carte
19b Motcomb St, SW1
⊖ Knightsbridge
☎ 020 7235 0596
cosmeticsalacarte.com
✇ 10/K13

Footopia
Peter Jones, Sloane Sq, SW1
⊖ Sloane Square
☎ 020 7259 0845
peterjones.co.uk
✇ 14/K14

Groom
49 Beauchamp Pl, SW3
⊖ Knightsbridge
☎ 020 7581 1248
groomlondon.com
✇ 10/I13

Hugh & Stephen
161 Ebury St, SW1
⊖ Sloane Square
☎ 020 7730 2196
✇ 14/L14

Jo Hansford
19 Mount St, W1
⊖ Bond Street
☎ 020 7495 7774
johansford.com
✇ 10/K10

John Frieda
4 Aldford St, W1
⊖ Bond Street
☎ 020 7491 0840
johnfrieda.com
✇ 10/K10

Lockonego
394 King's Rd, SW10
⊖ Sloane Square
☎ 020 7795 1798
lockonego.com
✇ 14/K14

Margaret Dabbs
36 Weymouth St, W1
⊖ Baker Street
☎ 020 7487 5510
margaretdabbs.co.uk
✇ 6/L6

Nails Inc
41 South Molton St, W1
⊖ Bond Street
☎ 020 7499 8333
nailsinc.com
✇ 6/L-M8

The Nail Lounge
1 Kingly Court,
Kingly St, W1
⊖ Piccadilly Circus
☎ 020 7287 1847
thenaillounge.com
✇ 7/N9

Nicky Clarke
130 Mount St, W1
⊖ Bond Street
☎ 0844 8848 888
nickyclarke.com
✇ 10/K10

Otylia Roberts
142 Wigmore St, W1
⊖ Bond Street
☎ 020 7486 5537
otyliaroberts.co.uk
✇ 6/K8

Real Hair
6 Cale St, SW3
⊖ Sloane Sq
☎ 020 7589 0877
realhair.co.uk
⊕ 14/H15

Strip
112 Talbot Rd, W11
⊖ Westbourne Park
☎ 020 7727 2754
2strip.com
⊕ 5/C7

Vaishaly Patel
51 Paddington St, W1
⊖ Baker Street
☎ 020 7224 6088
vaishaly.com
⊕ 6/K6

St James's Beauty Clinic
13 Strutton Ground, SW1
⊖ St James's Park
☎ 020 7222 8442
stjamesbeauty.com
⊕ 11/O13

Trevor Sorbie
27 Floral St, WC2
⊖ Covent Garden
☎ 0870 920 1103
trevorsorbie.com
⊕ 7/Q9

Xfolia
52 Lambs Conduit St, WC1
⊖ Holborn
☎ 020 7242 5749
xfolia.com
⊕ 7/R6

Gentleman's hour

F. Flittner
86 Moorgate, EC2
⊖ Moorgate
☎ 020 7606 4750
fflittner.com
⊕ 8/X7

Geo. F. Trumper
9 Curzon St, W1
⊖ Green Park
☎ 020 7499 1850
trumpers.com
⊕ 10/L11

Truefitt & Hill
71 St James's St, SW1
⊖ Green Park
☎ 020 7493 2961
truefittandhill.com
⊕ 11/N10

08

Gentlemen's Tonic
31a Bruton Place, W1
⊖ Green Park
☎ 020 7297 4343
gentlemenstonic.com
⊕ 6/M9

Murdock London
340 Old St, EC1
⊖ Old Street
☎ 020 7729 2288
murdocklondon.com
⊕ 4-8/X5

Wholeman
67 New Bond St, W1
⊖ Bond Street
☎ 020 7629 6659
wholeman.co.uk
⊕ 6/M8

Gyms and health clubs

100 Club
100 Oxford St, W1
⊖ Oxford Circus
(020 7636 0933
the100club.co.uk
⊕ 6/K8

GymBox
St Martins Lane Hotel,
42 St Martin's Lane, WC2
⊖ Leicester Square
(020 7395 0270
gymbox.co.uk
⊕ 7/P9

Matt Roberts
16 Berkeley St, W1
⊖ Green Park
(020 7491 9989
personaltrainer.uk.com
⊕ 10/M10

**Catalyst Health and
Fitness**
30 Bury St, SW1
⊖ Green Park
(020 7930 0742
catalysthealth.com
⊕ 7/Q7

The Hurlingham Club
Ranelagh Gdns, SW6
⊖ Putney Bridge
(020 7736 8411
hurlinghamclub.org.uk
⊕ Off map

Pineapple Dance Studios
7 Langley St, WC2
⊖ Covent Garden
(020 7836 4004
pineapple.uk.com
⊕ 7/Q9

Chelsea Harbour Club
Watermeadow Lane, SW6
⊖ Fulham Broadway
(020 7371 7700
harbourclubchelsea.com
⊕ Off map

KXGym
151 Draycott Ave, SW3
⊖ South Kensington
(020 7584 5333
kxgym.com
⊕ 14/I15

The Place
17 Duke's Rd, WC1
⊖ Euston
(020 7121 1090
theplace.org.uk
⊕ 3/P4

Danceworks
16 Balderton St, W1
⊖ Bond Street
(020 7629 6183
danceworks.co.uk
⊕ 6/L9

Lambton Place
Westbourne Grove, W11
⊖ Notting Hill Gate
(020 7229 2291
lambton.co.uk
⊕ 5/C8

The Third Space
13 Sherwood St, W1
⊖ Piccadilly Circus
(020 7439 6333
thethirdspace.com
⊕ 7/N9

Inner peace

Body Control Pilates
35 Little Russell St, WC1
🚇 Tottenham Court Rd
📞 020 7636 8900
bodycontrol.co.uk
✛ 7/Q7

Parliament Hill Lido
Parliament Hill, NW3
🚇 Belsize Park
📞 020 7485 3873
✛ Off map

The Serpentine
Hyde Park, SW7
🚇 High St Kensington
📞 020 7706 3422
serpentinelido.com
✛ 10/I10

Calmia
52 Marylebone High St, W1
🚇 Baker Street
📞 0845 009 2450
calmia.com
✛ 6/L6

Porchester Baths
The Porchester Centre,
Queensway, W2
🚇 Queensway
📞 020 7792 3980
✛ 5/E7

Triyoga
6 Erskine Rd, NW3
🚇 Chalk Farm
📞 020 7483 3344
triyoga.co.uk
✛ Off map

Hampstead Bathing Ponds
Hampstead Heath NW3
🚇 Hampstead
📞 020 7845 3873
✛ Off map

Portobello Yoga
The Ladbroke Rooms,
2c Exmoor St, W10
🚇 Ladbroke Grove
📞 020 8960 0846
theladbrokerooms.com
✛ Off map

Yohm
32 Paultons Sq, SW3
🚇 Sloane Square
📞 020 7795 1888
yohm.co.uk
✛ Off map

08

Oasis
32 Endell St, WC2
🚇 Covent Garden
outdoorswimming
society.com
✛ 7/Q8

Royal Automobile Club
89 Pall Mall, SW1
🚇 Piccadilly Circus
📞 020 7930 2345
royalautomobileclub.co.uk
✛ 11/O11

York Hall Baths
Old Ford Rd, E2
🚇 Bethnal Green
📞 020 8980 2243
✛ Off map

See page 9
to scan the
directory

PROPERTY HOT SPOTS
FOR FINE LIVING

Fournier Street, E1

Previous page: Little Venice, W9

An Englishman's home has always been his castle, so buying a house or flat rather than simply renting is an idea deeply embedded in the national psyche. Since London is a sprawling city, diversity is the key where edgy neighbourhoods exist side by side with well established, luxurious ones. Delightful as it would be to own a townhouse on Eaton Square, other parts of London present better value and more discreet charm. Some are 'new' or up-and-coming, others are just beautiful houses in chic neighbourhoods.

East End glamour

In the City, for example, areas like **Clerkenwell** are now the preserve of a compatible mixture of media types, city traders and loft living enthusiasts. **Smithfields Market** forms the backbone of this burgeoning area and the most charming streets are those around the church of St Bartholomew the Great, such as **Bartholomew Passage** and **Close**. Also highly prized is the impressive Georgian **Charterhouse Square**. If your budget won't stretch to a house here the fabulously curvaceous Art Deco Florin Court consider a slightly more affordable addition to the square.

09

Columbia Road
Flower Market, E2

Far east

The 2012 London Olympics should bring a multitude of benefits to London and one of the first signs of this has been the rising property prices in little-known areas out to the east. **Stratford**, **Hackney** and **Bethnal Green**, areas that were previously avoided by anyone who could afford to live elsewhere, have become the areas of choice for the savvy property investor. The further development of the East London tube line and the siting of the Stratford International Eurostar terminal will help to consolidate the Olympic boost. While they have yet to become chic neighbourhoods in themselves, these are the places to watch for investment growth over the coming decade.

Further east, in the heart of originally industrial **Spitalfields**, lies the historically fascinating **Fournier Street** built for Huguenot silk workers in the early 18th century, some full of Georgian houses retain original shuttering and panelling. **Wilkes Street** and **Princelet Street** are in a similar mould and are often used as a location for films of a suitably gritty Dickensian nature. The atmosphere is cool and alternative. To the east are the vibrant and ethnically diverse **Brick Lane** and **Columbia Road**; the core of **Shoreditch**'s retro boutiques are within striking distance.

Northeast cachet

Islington, made famous by Tony Blair in the 1990s, is home to unsung areas **Canonbury** and **Barnsbury**, to the east and west of Upper Street respectively. **Alwyne Place**, **Canonbury Square**, **Colebrook Row** and **Willow Bridge Road** are Canonbury's star turns, preservation requirements have ensured that many of the Georgian townhouses have remained as single homes rather than flats. Barnsbury is similarly swathed in aesthetically pleasing properties; **Milner Square**, **Lonsdale Square**, **Barnsbury Square**, **Ripplevale Grove**, **Richmond Crescent** and the quaintly proportioned **Mathilda Street** are the key addresses here. In both areas, locked garden squares hint at delightful open spaces accessible only to residents.

09

Colebrook Row, N1

Nearby, the redevelopment of once insalubrious **King's Cross** has opened up a large tract of central London. Although there are many new builds here, **Regent Quarter**, a surprisingly successful mix of Georgian, Victorian and state-of-the-art contemporary housing, is the pick of the crop so far. Quaint **Keystone Crescent** and **Northdown Street** form the core of existing options. South of Euston Road, 'North Bloomsbury' is benefiting, too, with wonderfully Art Deco mansion blocks around **Judd Street** and **Cromer Street** being reclaimed from student housing.

Southeast regeneration

Heading south of the river, regeneration has been gathering pace around London Bridge and SE1. Streets abutting **Borough Market** are in a heavenly spot for gastronomes; to the east, **Trinity Church Square** and **Merrick Square** are tranquil Georgian enclaves amid electic bustle. Towards the river, the evocatively named **Clink Street** is a narrow passageway dating in part from the 16th century. The nearby Tate Modern and splendid Shakespeare's Globe theatre bring the area rapidly up-to-date, and nestled beside them along **New Globe Walk** are numerous new property developments with notable river views.

09

Clink Street, SE1

Central classics

Back on the north bank, **Westminster** has few exciting options, the exception being the homogenously presented **Smith Square** and the streets that lead from it. Regular evening concerts held in St John's church help perpetuate the genteel atmosphere of this early 18th-century square. Further west lies **Pimlico**, once full of studio apartments known locally as bed-sitters but now emerging as if from a cocoon. Classic white Victorian terraces are the form here. **Eccleston Square**, with tennis court in the private garden is most desirable, but anywhere within The Grid, from **Alderney Street** to **Westmoreland Terrace** is promising.

Fitzrovia, squarely situated in the West End, is overlooked as a residential area. For such a central spot prices are affordable when compared to Covent Garden, Bloomsbury or Mayfair, and streets around **Charlotte Street** are best. Developed erratically, it is less architecturally cohesive than its neighbours, and so has never enjoyed such stratospheric pricing. Packed with offices, shops and entertainment, its charms lie not in its tranquillity but in its location, just seconds north of Oxford Street.

Adjacent to Fitzrovia, **Marylebone** is hardly a new discovery but is resolutely attractive and unerringly chic. **Marylebone High Street** is as vibrant as ever,

09

Ultimate cachet

It's impossible not to mention the prime areas of central London where armies of clean, stucco-fronted houses can be found. **Mayfair**, **Belgravia**, **Kensington**, **Holland Park**, **Notting Hill** and **Chelsea** are unilaterally popular. Discreet pockets of wonderfulness – a private garden like **Ladbroke Square**, a miniature terraced house in **Farm Street** or quaint cobbled mews like **Wilton Row** – offer some of the most attractive housing in London.

Areas to watch include the seedier edges of Belgravia towards Victoria, as the coach station moves out, and the shabby yet central areas of Bayswater and Lancaster Gate where the Notting Hill Gate, effect is knocking on.

Wilton Row, SW1

and the area as a whole harbours some of the prettiest mews houses in London. **Devonshire Mews**, **Devonshire Place Mews** and **Beaumont Mews** are some examples. North of Marylebone Road, the area around Marylebone station, is less chic, but its proximity to Marylebone High Street renders it attractive to those with shallower pockets. **Dorset Square** and the streets around **Ivor Place** are the jewels in this area of town.

Northwest tranquillity

Maida Vale and **Little Venice** are underappreciated by a majority of Londoners. The former is a haven of mansion blocks à la Hercule Poirot, while the latter is populated by smart, white mansions set on spacious streets or crescents. The canal and the predominance of secret communal gardens adds to the peaceful air. In Maida Vale, streets fronting Paddington Recreation Ground are in demand, as are apartments on Castellain or Lauderdale Mansions. In Little Venice, Randolph Crescent is unfailingly smart, as are Randolph Road, Clarendon Gardens and canal side Blomfield Road.

09

Relocation agents

Dovetail Relocation
020 8673 8026
dovetailrelocation.com

Relocation Assist
020 8398 5663
relocationassist.co.uk

UK Relocation
020 8442 0044
ukrelocation.com

House hunters

Annabel Stoner
020 8877 1808
annabelstoner.com

Khalil & Kane
020 7222 2622
khalilandkane.com

Quintessentially Estates
020 7758 3331
quintessentiallyestates.com

Crofton & Associates
020 7832 5858
croftonandassociates.com

London Property Finders
020 7493 4355
londonpropertyfinders.co.uk

Templeton Property
07801 465 522
templetonproperty.co.uk

Londonwide estate agents

Hamptons
020 7584 2044
hamptons.co.uk

John D. Wood
020 7908 1110
johndwood.co.uk

Lane Fox
020 7499 4785
lanefox.co.uk

Harrods
020 7225 6508
harrods.com/estates

Knight Frank
020 7629 8171
knightfrank.co.uk

Savills
020 7581 5234
savills.co.uk

Rentals and serviced apartments

10 Park Street
020 7529 0990
pauldavieslondon.com

Beaufort House
020 7584 2600
beauforthouse.co.uk

Grand Residence Club
0800 221 222
grandresidenceclub.com

The Apartments
020 7589 3271
theapartments.co.uk

Flemings Mayfair
020 7499 2964
flemings-mayfair.co.uk

London Perfect
020 7938 2939
londonperfect.com

Luxury property developers

Candy & Candy
℡ 020 7594 4300
candyandcandy.com

Spink Property
℡ 020 8380 0808
spinkproperty.co.uk

Yoo
℡ 020 7009 0100
yoo.com

Interior designers

Kelly Hoppen
℡ 020 7471 3350
kellyhoppen.com

Nina Campbell
℡ 020 7471 4270
ninacampbell.com

Thorp Design
10 Peterborough Mews, SW6
⊖ Parsons Green
℡ 020 7731 6887
thorp.co.uk
⊕ Off map

Nicolas Haslam
℡ 0207 730 8623
nicholashaslam.com

Target Living
6 Burnsall St, SW3
⊖ Sloane Sq
℡ 020 7351 7588
targetliving.com
⊕ 14/I16

Todhunter Earle
79-89 Lots Rd, SW10
⊖ Sloane Square
℡ 020 7349 9999
todhunterearle.com
⊕ Off map

Star architects

Foster and Partners
℡ 020 7738 0455
fostcrandpartners.com

John Pawson
℡ 020 7837 2929
johnpawson.com

Rogers Stirk Harbour and Partners
℡ 020 7385 1235
rsh-p.com

09

Further London property sources

Country Life
London wide property
countrylife.co.uk

Primelocation
London wide property
primelocation.com

The London Property Guide
By Carrie Seagrave

See page 9
to scan the
directory

ELITE LIFESTYLE
SERVICES

Harrods
87-135 Brompton Road, SW1

Previous page: Wild at Heart
222 Westbourne Grove, W11

For the happy few with limitless budgets but limited time, it makes sense to engage the city's fabulous elite service companies to do your bidding. Forget the drudgery of food shopping or ticket booking and think lifestyle management. Helicopter from Heathrow? No problem. Seasonally organised shoes? No problem. Home hairdressing and massage? Easy. As ever, it's not really what you know, but whom you know in this domain.

Making an entrance

For those who regard simple London living with some disdain, there's always a way around the mundane basics. Fresh off the plane or train, what could be more luxurious than a helicopter to chauffeur you to your pied à terre? Ever forging ahead with its dedication to bespoke living, **Harrods Aviation** has a fabulously chic service that wings clients to central London in the blink of an eye. Such an entry to the Big Smoke certainly sets the right tone for basking in the high life. But if taking in the sights is what you crave, try a **Heli Tour**. Away from the irascible bustle, the aerial view of the cityscape is the way to go for those keen to spread their wings and escape.

10

Practical Princess
39 Stephendale Road, SW6

Lifestyle management

For the ultimate in luxury living, **Quintessentially**, the concierge company set up to cater for the needs of the cash-rich-time-poor, is a one-stop-shop favoured by high-profile types like Madonna, Gwyneth Paltrow, and movie mogul Harvey Weinstein. It's akin to a global members club and guarantees to cater to the every whim of its members, no matter how particular. London was its original home, and despite having expanded cross-continentally, London remains the hub.

Club Concierge is another outfit that arranges exclusive access to elite events and places, such as film premières, members' clubs, select night spots, and offers a means of securing boxes not only at highbrow cultural venues such as the Royal Opera House, but also at high-profile sporting events like Ascot.

Personal shopping

Erika Gibbs, of **Practical Princess**, is another seasoned lifestyle manager who gives a unique personal service to ensure the smooth running of the daily life of a number of A-list clients. One ingenious service (alongside others including personal shopping, wardrobe assessment, and event planning) is its shoe management service. Clients have her shoes arranged by style, material and season, and then they

10

are snapped and documented in a database, so when you can't locate your Jimmy Choo slingbacks, Gibbs can check her files and tell you which wardrobe, in which of your houses, in which country they are in.

Other amazing personal shoppers with the sartorial edge include **Laura Campbell**, **Sheila Bathurst**, and **Caroline Stanbury**. When nothing but shopping is on the agenda, these fashion gurus whisk the style savvy from boutique to fashion emporium, picking out the latest season's scene stealer, perfectly suited to the shape and tastes of their client.

Quintessentially Driven
quintessentially.com/driven

Harrods, **Selfridges** and **Topshop** have their own in-house personal shoppers, service is more often than not complimentary. They can be a godsend when the slew of concessions under one roof can seem over-whelming. After a brief consultation these personal shoppers, who know the wares and trinkets of their individual stores inside out and back to front, make a beeline for the items it would have taken you years of trawling through racks of clothes to find.

Chauffeured service

The bicycle is one way to get ahead of the crowd. If you have your own set of wheels keep **Scooterman** on speed dial. This nifty service sees a man on mini wheels come to the aid of the sleep-deprived or inebriated. On arrival he pops his scooter in the trunk of the car and drives the world-weary home. **Green Tomato Cars** provides environmentally friendly cars with driver, but if you can't do without your Rolls or limousine, you can hire one with chauffeur from **Quintessentially Driven**.

Silver service

If the occasion calls for a party of sublime proportions, once again Practical Princess's Erika Gibbs *(see page 173)* is the woman to call. If you like to work your own magic but are less keen to work the room with mountains of canapés and champagne, call in a crack

10

Scooterman
scooterman.co.uk.

silver service team from either **At Your Service** or the **Admirable Crichton** (a sobriquet purloined from the J.M. Barrie comedy). **Audiosushi** should be able to help with the music – by casting a discerning eye over the music on your iPod, it ascertains what you should be listening to and adds a selection of tunes that complement existing downloads. If the gathering is more intimate outdoor, call on picnic-in-the-park specialists, **Chef 2 U**. Its Picnic 2 U hampers are brilliant for summer events such as the opera seasons at Glyndebourne or Garsingston.

Flowers for every occasion

For floral decoration (also handy should you wish to graciously send a posy to thank a host), remember **Jane Packer**, **Wild at Heart** and **McQueens**. The masters of beautiful bouquets that'll brighten any venue.

Grooming chez vous

Finally, elite relaxation is key to any sojourn in London. From the comfort of your chosen abode, call **Unlisted London**, which has a Rolodex of pampering professionals at its command, ready to be dispatched at the click of a finger. **The Powder Puff Girls** are experts at applying as is **Skin Deep**, while for manicures, try **Nails at Work**. For that sun-kissed glow, **Vanair** is just the thing: a makeup St Tropez spray-tanning booth that comes right to your door. And when the parties are over, relax with the pummelling pros from **Cadence Massage** – there's nothing like a personal massage at home to iron out the worries of the world.

10

Paula Pryke Flowers, Liberty,
Great Marlborough Street, W1

Making an entrance

EBG Helicopters
(01737 823 282
ebghelicopters.co.uk

Harrods Aviation
(01279 660 800
harrodsaviation.com

Heli Tours
(020 8953 4411
cabairhelicopters.com

Lifestyle management

Club Concierge
(01707 259481
club-concierge.com

Cushion the Impact
(020 7704 6922
cushiontheimpact.co.uk

Quintessentially
quintessentially.com

Personal shopping

Caroline Stanbury
(07795 420 646
style-me.net

Harrods
87 Brompton Rd, SW1
⊖ Knightsbridge
(020 7730 1234
harrods.com/
byappointment
⊕ 10/I13

Practical Princess
39 Stephendale Rd, SW6
⊖ Parsons Green
(020 7371 0276
practicalprincess.net
⊕ Off map

Fenwick
63 New Bond St, W1
⊖ Bond Street
(020 7629 9161
fenwick.co.uk
⊕ 6/M8

Harvey Nichols
109 Knightsbridge, SW1
⊖ Knightsbridge
(020 7235 5000
harveynicols.com
⊕ 10/J12

Selfridges
400 Oxford St, W1
⊖ Bond Street
(020 7318 3536
selfridges.com
⊕ 6/K8

Flair
(01189 260 405
flairstyle.co.uk

**Laura Campbell and
Sheila Bathurst**
(07944 566860
campbellandbathurst.
com

Topshop
Oxford Circus, W1
⊖ Oxford Circus
(020 7636 7700
topshop.com
⊕ 7/N8

10

Chauffered London

Addison Lee
© 020 7387 8888
addisonlee.com

Green Tomato Cars
© 020 8568 0022
greentomatocars.com

Scooterman
© 0870 242 6999
scooterman.co.uk

Drive-U-Home
© 020 7880 1100
driveuhome.co.uk

Quintessentially Driven
© 0870 383 3555
quintessentially.com/
driven

Virgin Limobike
© 020 7930 0814
virgin.com/subsites/
virginlimobike

Silver service

Admirable Crichton
© 020 7326 3800
admirable-crichton.co.uk

At Your Service
© 020 7610 8610
ays.co.uk

Chef 2 U
© 020 7370 1997
chef2u.co.uk

Alexander Events
© 020 7731 0878
alexander-events.com

Audiosushi
© 0870 9770 025
audiosushi.net

Imperial Staff
17 Radley Mews, W8
High St Kensington
© 020 7795 6255
staffofdistinction.co.uk
⊕ 13/D14

Grooming chez vous

Cadence Massage
© 07879 852288
cadencemassage.com

The Powder Puff Girls
© 020 7480 5094
thepowderpuffgirls.com

Unlisted London
© 0870 2255 007
unlistedlondon.com

Nails at Work
nailsatwork.co.uk

Skin Deep
© 07932 020840
beautyinyourhome.com

Vanair
© 07956 417873
vanair.co.uk

Flowers for every occasion

Black Tulip
28 Exmouth Market, EC1
⊖ Farringdon
☎ 020 7689 0068
theblacktulip.co.uk
⊕ 3/T5

Jane Packer
32 New Cavendish St, W1
⊖ Oxford Circus
☎ 020 7935 2673
jane-packer.co.uk
⊕ 6/L7

Paula Pryke Flowers
Liberty, Great
Marlborough St, W1
⊖ Oxford Circus
☎ 020 7573 9563
paula-pryke-flowers.com
⊕ 6/N8

Dansk flowers
124 Wandsworth Bridge
Rd, SW6
⊖ Parsons Green
☎ 020 7736 6353
danskflowers.co.uk
⊕ Off map

McQueens
70 Old St, EC1
⊖ Old Street
☎ 020 7251 5505
mcqueens.co.uk
⊕ 4-8/X5

Wild at Heart
222 Westbourne Grove,
W11.
⊖ Notting Hill Gate
☎ 020 7727 3095
wildatheart.com
⊕ 5/C8

10

See page 9
to scan the
directory

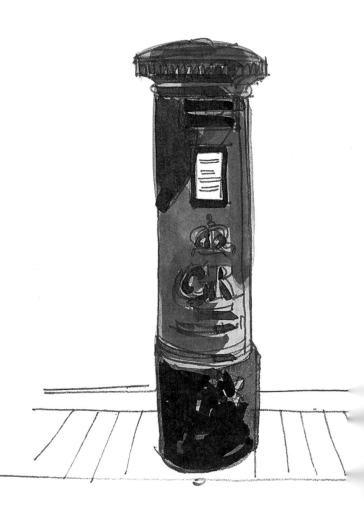

INDEX

11

11

11

11

Transport
for London

Congestion
charging

Central
ZONE

11

193

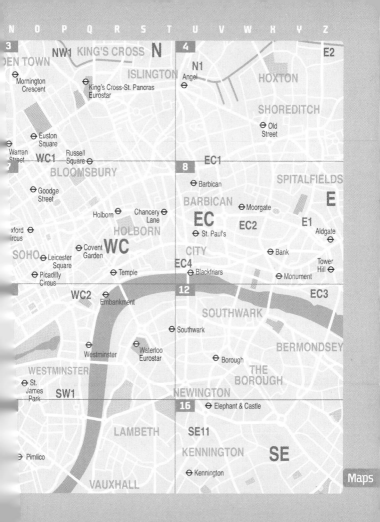

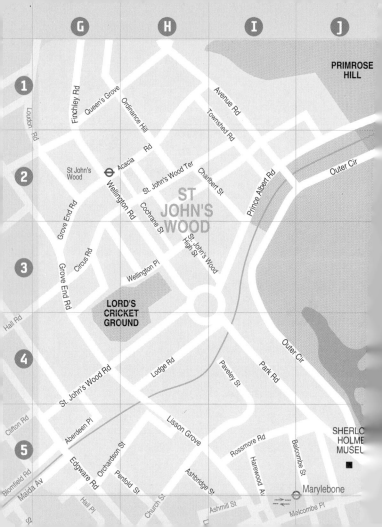

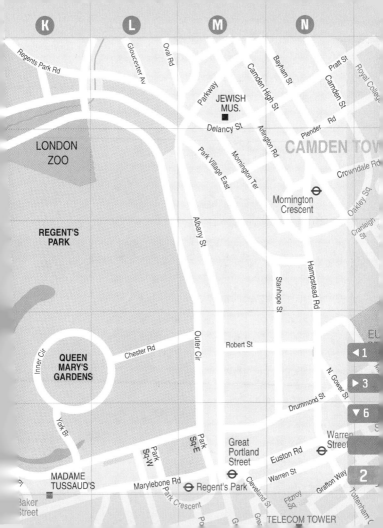

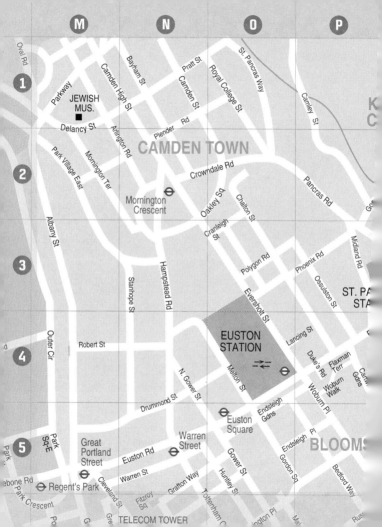

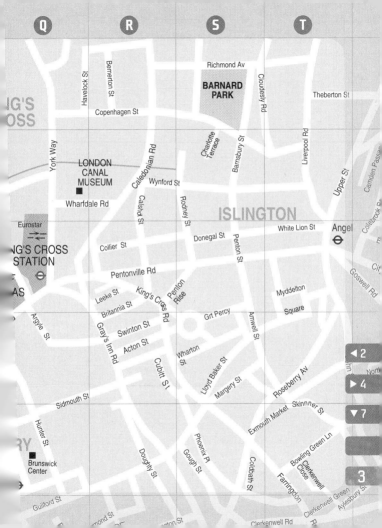

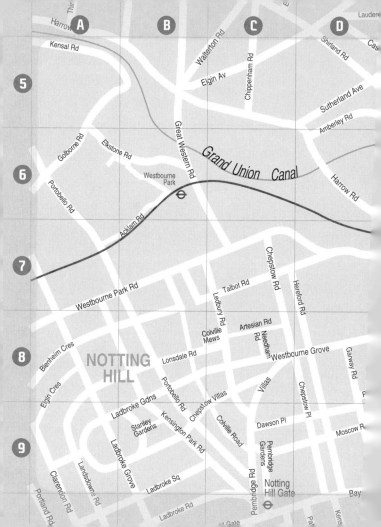

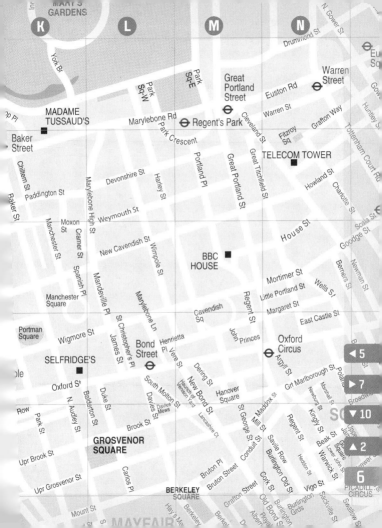

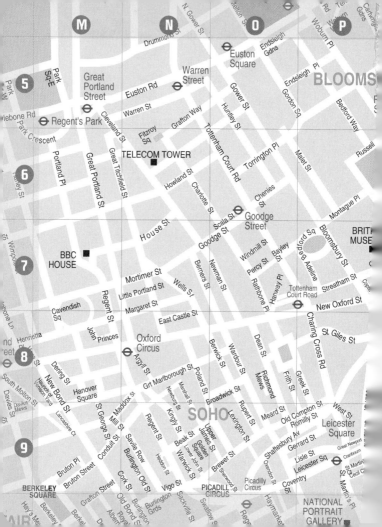

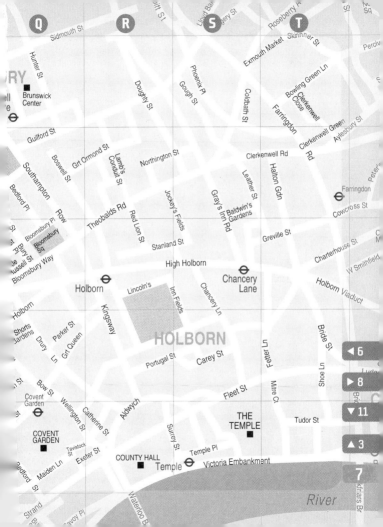

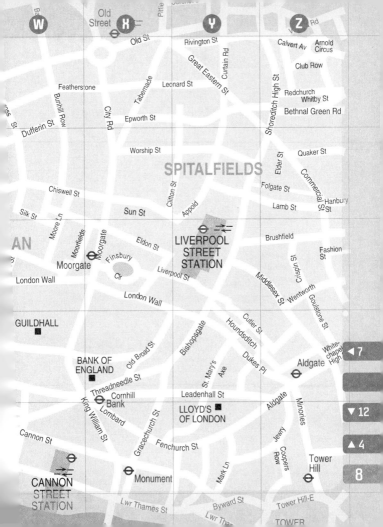

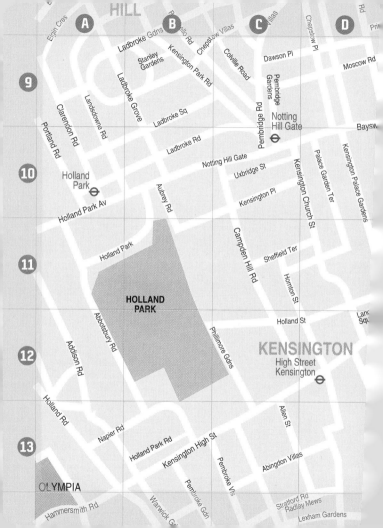

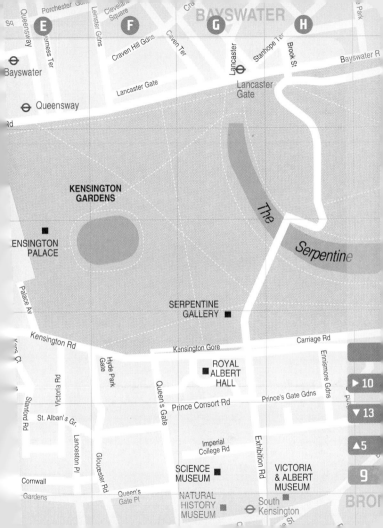

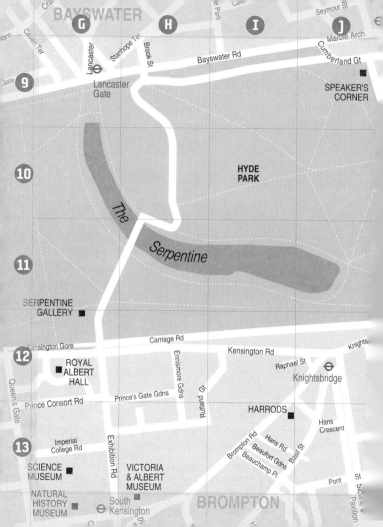

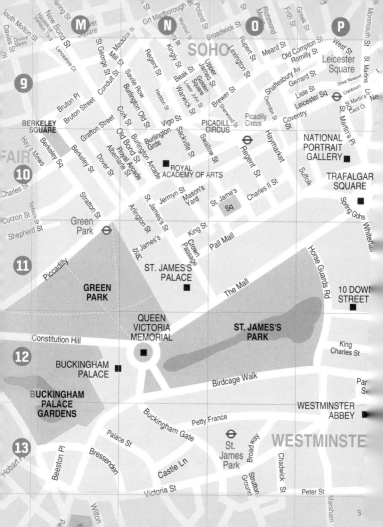

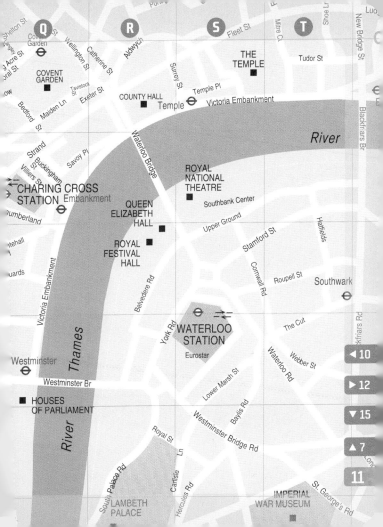

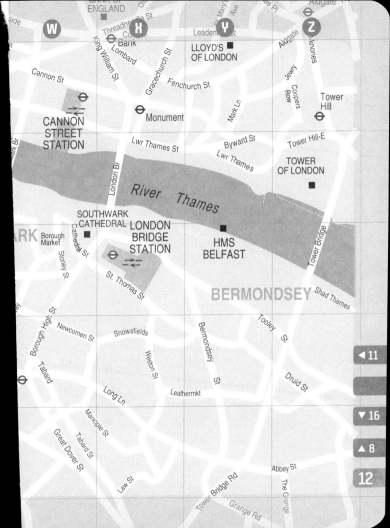

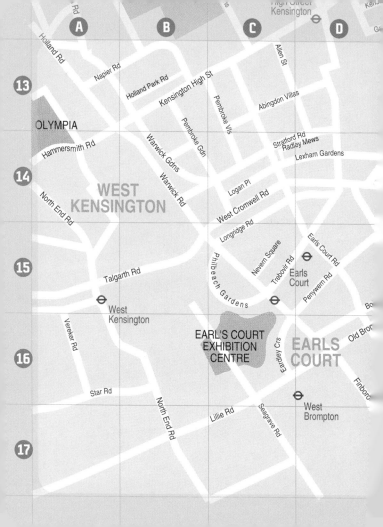

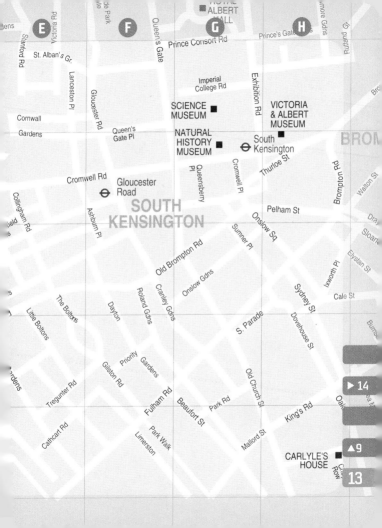

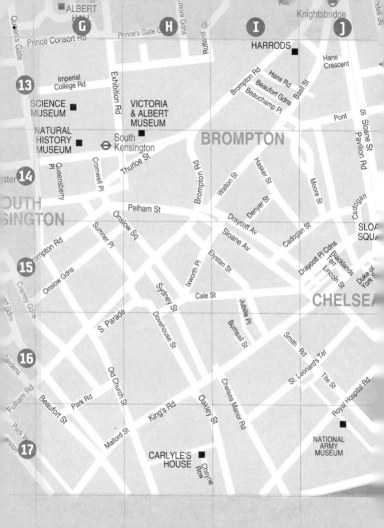

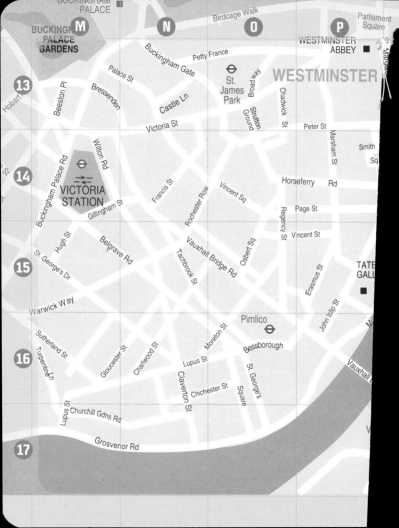

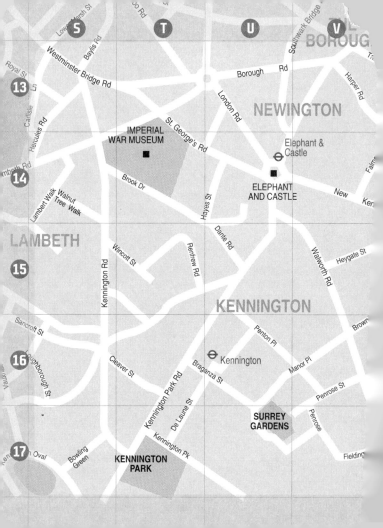

LONDON UN

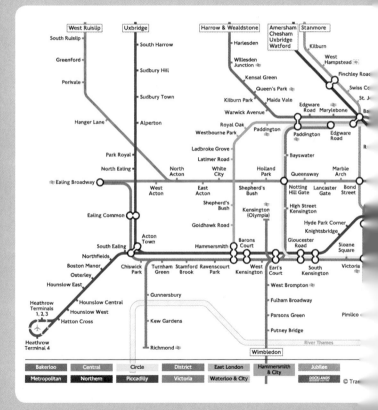

DERGROUND

OTHER TITLES IN THE AUTHENTIK COLLECTION

Europe
Gourmet London
Artistik London

Gourmet Paris
Chic Paris
Artistik Paris

FORTHCOMING AUTHENTIK GUIDES – SPRING 2008

North America
Gourmet New York
Chic New York
Artistik New York

Europe
Barcelona
Berlin
Milan
Prague

Asia
Beijing

FORTHCOMING WINE ROADBOOKS – AUTUMN 2008

France
Bordeaux
Burgundy
Champagne
Loire Valley

Italy
Tuscany

Spain
Rioja

North America
Napa Valley
Sonoma County

Visit www.authentikbooks.com
to find out more about **AUTHENTIK** ® titles

Ⓚ

Beatrice Hodgkin

After a risqué induction to the world of journalism by way of the *Erotic Review*, Beatrice now applies her scribbling skills to features for *Easy Living* magazine and cultural websites such as www.thefirstpost.co.uk and www.kultureflash.net. Reviewing sophisticated, happening places gives her free reign to swan around London like a lady of leisure, having far too much fun. And all in the name of work.

Alain Bouldouyre

Gentleman artist Alain Bouldouyre captures in his fine line drawings what our *Chic London* author conjures up in words – the quintessence of the city. Art director for *Senso* magazine, author and illustrator of numerous Art books and guides, Alain fast tracks around the world, his hand-stitched loafers – paintbox and sketch pad his most precious accessories.

COMMERCIAL LICENSING
Authentik illustrations, text and listings are available for commercial licensing at www.authentikartwork.com

ORIGINAL ARTWORK
All signed and numbered original illustrations by Alain Bouldouyre published in this book are available for sale. Original artwork by Alain Bouldouyre is delivered framed with a certificate of authenticity.

CUSTOM-MADE EDITIONS
Authentik books make perfect, exclusive gifts for personal or corporate purposes.

Special editions, including personalized covers, excerpts from existing titles and corporate imprints, can be custom produced.

All enquiries should be addressed to Wilfried LeCarpentier at wl@authentikbooks.com

AUTHENTIK ®

K